FASHION *IN ACTION*

A series of concise, approachable books about current, global issues around fashion, offering readers guidance on how to become active participants in its future, and acting as calls to action.

BOOKS IN THE SERIES

Slow, by Hazel Clark
Appropriation, by Benjamin Linley Wild
Failure, by Nick Rees-Roberts
Animal, by Simona Segre-Reinach

PREFACE

I sit writing, listening to the comforting hum of bees, care of an episode of the BBC "Slow Radio" podcast. The Slow Research Lab and the Bureau for Listening similarly invite me and "all in the world," to engage in slow listening.[1] Slow Living LDN encourages me to "live better, not faster,"[2] and TikTok videos inform me how to do so. Haemin Sunim's popular book, *The Things You Can Only See When You Slow Down* (with 3 million copies sold, according to its cover) rests reassuringly on my desk. Beside me are other scholarly and general books, that directly address "slow," all published since 2001, stacked in a growing pile. The latest, *Slow Down* by Kōhei Saitō, is a manifesto for degrowth, a tactic to which we will return. I have just finished eating a Slow Food-inspired lunch comprised of items grown as closely as possible to where I live. All of which attest to the increasing, and wide-ranging, interest in *slow*. It is a concept that appeared no more than forty years ago, which appeals in a world that appears to have lost its equilibrium.

Slow emerged from the Slow Food Movement that began in 1986 in Italy to promote traditional and regional cuisine, local ecosystems, and the pleasure and nourishing effect of food. It is neither surprising nor inappropriate that slow food practices should be pivotal to this book, which calls for action towards change for fashion. Traditionally, no matter in which culture or society, all human beings need food, places to shelter, and clothing. While the concept of *slow* began with food, and then impacted cities, it has been adopted increasingly as a conceptual framework for reflecting on how we live, as well as on what we wear. In large part, it is a response to the "fast life." Shaped by industrial civilization, rooted in modernity, globalization, and in the information society, people have become separated from simple pleasures in many aspects of their life, including, curiously enough, in the agency they bring to fashioning and dressing themselves. All of this came into sharp focus in December 2019, when the identification of the coronavirus disease in Wuhan, China, began a global pandemic that proved fatal for nearly 7 million people. This book was developed and written substantially during the years that followed when the whole world literally slowed down. As the pandemic prevented movement, the practice of slow living was effectively imposed worldwide. With lockdowns, and people working from home for safety, everyday life took on a greater sense of importance. Ideas of degrowth, and of sufficiency, as endorsed by nineteenth-century writer Henry David Thoreau, and practiced by the North American Voluntary Simplicity Movement, proved platforms for reflection.

Being at home did not erase relationships with fashion, but it made them more considered. As items remained unworn in wardrobes, the pandemic caused many people to rethink how they consumed clothes and the number of items they needed. The "zoom shirt" became a neologism, for the garment that was kept on the back of a desk chair to enable the wearer to quickly look presentable during ubiquitous online communications. Sartorially, the pandemic fostered slower, more caring attitudes to how clothing decisions were made, paying greater attention to feelings of comfort. Fashion manufacturing slowed down, as global supply chains were impacted by factories closing in China, Vietnam, and other East Asian locations. When the *Ever Given*, one of the world's largest cargo ships, ran aground in the Suez Canal for six days in March 2021, blocking all traffic, it felt like a metaphor for the worst of times. Yet if we view fashion through a slow lens, as a form of personal creativity and style not reliant on commerce and trade, our perspective changes to highlight the agency of wearers. Being able to choose what to wear is freeing and creative, and should not be dictated by a global, commercial, and profit-driven industry. For readers of this book, an investigation of *slow* for fashion (as distinct from "slow fashion") is offered as an ethical and creative response to the sense of disquiet and anxiety that, for many people, underlies choices about what they wear and how they dress, as well as their broader feelings about the world.

A few last observations ... *Slow* creates its own unique visual imagery through meaningful and sometimes playful contrasts between f/Fashion's lower and upper cases. Thinking slowly might require new word-pictures to challenge the definitive frame of the book itself. This is not to destroy the past, which cannot be undone. Instead, *Slow* is intended to become a learning process whereby we engage with our own reflections and realities. Welcome to the conversation.

Regina A. Root

SERIES EDITOR'S PREFACE

The *Fashion In Action* series responds directly to the upsurge of interest in critical issues in fashion—the industry, its ethics, its values, its contribution to global profits, its challenges amidst profound planetary change. When we choose what to wear, the connections we make might be understood as a chapter in a larger global fashion story. How do we re-imagine fashion as participants, encouraging a "freedom of thinking," while unraveling the past, challenging our present, and pointing to the future? This series goes beyond delineating global trends and fashion practices to imagine the very concepts of fashion anew. After all, we are planetary subjects in the making.

The words that you are about to experience in potentially sensory ways may very well inspire you to think differently about fashion. *Slow* invites us to fashion as a verb we might express unhurriedly, as in slowing down, in order to center the ethical nature of an industry that has too long been associated with waste and economic uncertainty. *Slow* praxis, Hazel Clark explains, advocates agency—and this implies an openness to new ways of thinking, making, doing, creating, questioning, learning, wearing—and thereby activities that also speak to the heart of *Fashion In Action.*

Each book in this series is divided into three parts and a Call to Action. "Speeding Up" grounds us in the present. How did we arrive at this historical juncture when unprecedented speed evokes the act of forgetting when we already know, through novelists and slow living activists and other sources, that slowness engages the art of remembering? When it comes to fashion, industrial narratives represent an obsolescence grounded in toxic waste and other exploitative practices. At some point brand names that once served as arbiters of consumer tastes and fashion knowledge, the author writes, gave way to increased access and technological reproduction under the guise of "fast fashion." Whether considering the likes of the rise of discardable fashion tourism or the realities of global textile waste in our oceans, what is it exactly that we are trying to throw away?

"Slowing Down" invites us to anticipate change through the lessons of the past. While "... fashion creates its own past through rapidly changing styles," it has equally represented what is overlooked, misinformed, innovative, and optimistic. The book engages disruptive aesthetics as a direction in the rebellion that makes up slow thinking in fashion. Creating pauses reveal what fashion might be. In the third section, "Redirection," these pauses, ways of knowing, and tactics become hopeful steps forward amidst planetary despair. Longer-term thinking ultimately requires a critical lens through which to engage an industry that frequently seems to put profits and its own growth ahead of people and the planet. "Redirection" speaks to what is heartfelt, intentional, and insightfully rebellious. It is, as *Slow* details, fashion WITH rather than for or about. Together with elements of self-care, sensorial knowledge, and the art of remembering, a new type of provenance might reveal a host of slow techniques, collaborative practices and listening and sharing designed to consider our reflections and creative rhythms.

Slow reminds us of the early optimism through which sustainable fashion initiatives engaged transcendent ways of thinking. The mindset to "use it and toss it," which has haunted fast fashion, leaves behind the forgetfulness of speed and embraces new concepts like "degrowth" and "sufficiency" within a more holistic or circular approach to fashion. From unworn items in our closet to fast fashion marketing, this book invites us to re-imagine the stories we are telling ourselves about fashion. Its final Call to Action offers a stunning alphabetical list with which to cultivate the new poetry that drives *Fashion In Action*.

SLOW

HAZEL CLARK

BLOOMSBURY VISUAL ARTS
LONDON • NEW YORK • OXFORD • NEW DELHI • SYDNEY

BLOOMSBURY VISUAL ARTS
Bloomsbury Publishing Plc, 50 Bedford Square, London, WC1B 3DP, UK
Bloomsbury Publishing Inc, 1359 Broadway, New York, NY 10018, USA
Bloomsbury Publishing Ireland, 29 Earlsfort Terrace, Dublin 2, Ireland

BLOOMSBURY, BLOOMSBURY VISUAL ARTS and the Diana logo
are trademarks of Bloomsbury Publishing Plc

First published in Great Britain 2026

Series design by Adriana Brioso
Cover image: Bennett Tobias/Unsplash

A catalogue record for this book is available from the British Library.

A catalog record for this book is available from the Library of Congress.

ISBN:	PB:	978-1-3502-5339-1
	ePDF:	978-1-3502-5340-7
	eBook:	978-1-3502-5341-4

Typeset by Integra Software Services Pvt. Ltd.
Printed and bound in India

For product safety related questions contact productsafety@bloomsbury.com.

To find out more about our authors and books visit www.bloomsbury.com
and sign up for our newsletters.

To Jacob

CONTENTS

ACKNOWLEDGMENTS

I am extremely grateful to Regina Root and Frances Arnold for encouraging my original proposal for this book, and for seeing it through with me, now as three editorial co-collaborators on the *Fashion In Action* series. It has been a *slow* process, but a good one. There are many other people whose thinking and writing proved fundamental to the development of this book, too many to name, but it would be remiss not to acknowledge the centrality of the related work of Kate Fletcher and Şölen Kipöz. Thanks to Parsons MA Fashion Studies students Avery Dove, and Wiktoria Gower, who read the manuscript and made helpful comments. As did Rachel Lifter, and so thoughtfully, at a point when it was "on the cutting room floor." And, once again, deepest thanks to Clive Dilnot, the toughest critic and most supportive champion.

INTRODUCTION

The seeds of this project were planted in 2006, when I was invited by design theorist Ezio Manzini to attend a "Slow + Design" symposium in Milan, organized by educators, design professionals, and members of the Italian Slow Food movement. The event built on a publication and exhibition by Manzini and François Jégou (2003), which can serve as a concise vision of thinking and doing sustainability in everyday lives.[1] The Milan symposium introduced the Slow Model as a way of behaving that would characterize new and potentially sustainable economies and ideas of wellbeing. A *Slow + Design Manifesto* (2006) was prepared for the symposium, describing the slow approach as one that offered the time to produce, appreciate, and cultivate quality. Ideologically, the point of departure was the Slow Food Movement, formally established in 1989, anecdotally in response to a proposal to locate a McDonald's near the Spanish Steps in Rome. Today, the movement continues to promote traditional and regional cuisine and local ecosystems, and the pleasure of food.

Writing in the 1990s, Czech author Milan Kundera responded to the growing sense of speed that many people felt was infiltrating their lives, with his fictional account *Slowness*. Weaving together philosophical ideas about modernity, technology, memory, and sensuality, he related parallel tales of seduction, staged on a midsummer's night, two centuries apart. In the process it is made clear how ideas of sensuality and pleasure changed as technology provided tools that demand our attention. Through his narrative, Kundera linked slowness to the act of remembering and speed to the (modern) act of forgetting. Journalist Carl Honoré noted how for Kundera speed could instill uncertainty, highlighting the importance of taking time for actions, events, people, our lives. His slow philosophy demanded balance, sometimes expressed as the musical term *tempo giusto* (literally "in exact time") or at the right speed.[2] In parallel, the global fashion system was producing more and more items within shorter time spans, as styles changed rapidly, creating enormous profits for the few, but producing greater material and human waste. A slow approach offered a possible direction for rethinking fashion.

Slow + fashion—a work in progress

In 1994, I presented a paper, "Eco Fashion—Conviction or Conceit?," motivated by the number of "ecology" inspired fashion collections that had appeared on international catwalks since 1989. While coincident with the emergence of the Slow Food Movement, "eco" and "green" were then the preferred terms being used in a fashion industry that, at the same time, was criticized for being strategic, superficial, and market centric. My conclusion was that while ecology had been referenced in fashion styles and images, the sustainable objectives of environmentalists were at odds with the economic growth-driven global fashion system.[3] To address the excess and waste being perpetuated, it was necessary to look outside it to explore the actual role of fashion in everyday life. One of the results was the anthology *Old Clothes New Looks Second Hand Fashion* (2005), co-edited with Alexandra Palmer. In it, authors explored secondhand clothes and practices historically, economically, culturally, and creatively, including beyond the Global North. By the time the book was published, wearing secondhand clothes as fashion was becoming more commonplace. It was a change I charted in my chapter on Hong Kong, where I had observed secondhand clothes starting to be fashionable and more culturally acceptable in the 1990s. The territory, then transitioning from being a British colony to being, in 1997, a Special Administrative Region (SAR) of China, was a fascinating crucible for studying local culture and practice, also explored by Ezio Manzini.

In 2003, Manzini and Jégou produced a book and exhibition that were informed by design workshops that had been held around the world. The first venue, in 2001, was the School of Design at the Hong Kong Polytechnic University, where I then worked. Although I was not directly involved in that project, Manzini's research on design and everyday life informed my thinking about design and cultural identity, and local fashion and dress in Hong Kong. Professor Manzini invited me to attend the 2006 Milan symposium as a scholar of fashion and dress, areas outside of his own expertise and of his project. The opportunity to learn about Slow + Design proved more enlightening and influential for me than I could have imagined. The timing of the symposium coincided with the publication of Wendy Parkins and Geoffrey Craig's *Slow Living,* a book which remains fundamental to understanding slow theory and practice. The authors significantly define slow living as,

> a process whereby everyday life—in all its pace and complexity, *frisson* and routine—is approached with care and attention, as subjects attempt to negotiate the different temporalities that they daily experience. It is above all an attempt to live in the present in a meaningful, sustainable, thoughtful *and pleasurable* way.[4]

All of the above were valuable lenses through which to consider the role of fashion in everyday life, and not only as a global commodity system. Contextualized by capitalism, the global fashion industry's unsustainable practices, massive waste, intensive energy use, and exploitation of human labor, plus the excessive consumption, which characterized fast fashion, were key points for reflection. But my interest was also in fashion's cultural role, and as a creative practice, a vehicle of communication and as a focus of action for wearers. These aspects all demanded more attention, not least in the context of exploring theories and practices of sustainment for fashion.

"Sustainable fashion" was conceptualized as a celebration of "ingenuity, self-awareness, and empowerment," by Regina Root, editor of a special issue of *Fashion Theory* on "Ecofashion" (Clark, 2008). Root framed the wider context for fashion relative to climate change, and the global decline in biodiversity. She referenced the, then recently released, documentary *An Inconvenient Tru*th (2007), featuring politician and Nobel Peace Laureate Al Gore, who explained the human impact of global warming. Contributing an article to the "Ecofashion" issue, I referenced three "lines of reflection" introduced at the Milan symposium, as significant to slow approaches to fashion. They were: the valuing of local resources and distributed economies; transparent production systems with less intermediation between producer and consumer; and sustainable and sensorial products that have a longer usable life and are more highly valued than typical "consumables."[5] Examples of smaller-scale fashion businesses in different regions, often run by women, were offered as approaches to a more ethical, caring, less wasteful and greedy fashion system. The question was posed as to whether a slow approach could be applied more systematically, or whether any attempt to do so was simply an oxymoron? My conclusion at that time was relatively optimistic, that slow + fashion (emphatically not *slow fashion*) could offer a redefined praxis for fashion (praxis is defined in this book as an active and theoretically informed practice). The article offered a number of examples, including Amy Twigger's *Keep and Share* project, mentioned next.

Keep and Share was featured in the exhibition *Well Fashioned: Eco Style in the U.K.* curated by Rebecca Earley at the Crafts Council Gallery in London in 2006. Described as "the first survey of high-end, well designed and made eco fashion design in the UK," the exhibition drew on research conducted by Earley since 2004 within the TED (Textiles Environment Design) Resource at Chelsea College of Art and Design. Rather than following previous similar presentations that focused on larger fashion labels, some displaying poor workmanship, and that omitted high end or couture items, *Well Fashioned* considered the manufacture, use, and disposal of clothing.

Praised by *International Herald Tribune* fashion journalist Suzy Menkes amongst others, it demonstrated the potentially influential position of exhibitions in reorienting fashion knowledge and practices. Earley hoped that visitors would leave as more informed consumers who, before making a purchase, asked themselves what it was they were buying, why they wanted it, how long they thought they would use it, and whether they could buy it from a more ethical outlet.[6] Endeavors that were featured, included Earley's *Top 100* project that upcycled and added value to a collection of blouses from a deceased owner. The TED Centre, where Earley worked, was innovative at the time in supporting research related to textiles, the environment, and design, much of it conducted by women, including PhD students. One was Kate Fletcher, who completed her dissertation in 1999, and went on to be a leading practice-based researcher, teacher, writer, and activist for environmental concerns in fashion. Fletcher has led the way in developing slow approaches.

Kate Fletcher was one of the first scholars to acknowledge slower forms of design in fashion, by documenting how clothing items have different temporal rhythms according to their practices of wear. Her *Lifetimes* project, conducted with Mathilda Tham in 2004, traced the different "lives" of four garments: a party top, basic underwear, utility trousers, and a plain coat, according to their use value and how much they were worn and laundered.[7] The Slow Food Movement served as Fletcher's conceptual point of departure for more sustainable models for fashion, as did the community-based ideas of Manzini and Jégou. In 2007, she defined a slow approach as being about "designing, producing, consuming and living better … [as] not time-based but quality-based." For Fletcher,

> Slow is not the opposite of fast—there is no dualism—but a different approach in which designers, buyers, retailers and consumers are more aware of the impacts of products on workers, communities and ecosystems.[8]

Fletcher cited eco-warrior Stewart Brand's vision of a more resilient human civilization based on achieving balance between different speeds and agendas, something which had become lost in the fashion industry. She shared my own questioning of the fashion system's emphasis on image, looking, and the "new," over the making and maintaining of physical material garments. In sum, to be sustainable, fashion could no longer prioritize the visual over the material. Most importantly, Fletcher expressed the view that slow culture provided an invitation to think about systems change in the fashion sector. It is a perspective that must lead, inevitably, to a questioning of the impact of the fashion system's underlying values. To achieve ethically driven change, the fashion sector must be contextualized as part of larger systems of economic, social, and environmental practices. A slow approach to fashion "represents a blatant discontinuity with the practices of today's sector; a break from the values and goals of fast (growth-based) fashion."[9] But, as I emphasize, the answer is not *slow fashion*, but *slow + fashion*. The "plus" sign between slow and fashion is important and needs explanation.

Slow + fashion—changing the discourse

Slow + fashion is the subject of this book, rather than "slow fashion," which has become a term overused in the media and by brands, ironically to sell more clothes. As Fletcher cautioned, *slow fashion* has been superficially represented and adopted, particularly by the fashion media as a descriptor for products that are "in some way less fast."[10] Separating "slow" and "fashion" with a "+" is not just semantic, it is intended to focus on slow as a form of fashion thinking and tactics, not a passing fashion movement or moment. In other words, it is a concept that demands action—by means of fashion praxis. Kate Fletcher's Local Wisdom project serves as an example. Conducted in nine countries, across three continents, the practice-based research (2008–18) highlighted wearing and tending to garments *in use*. In doing so it defined a view of fashion provision and expression that was not dependent on continuous consumption, but on the creativity, skills, and the choices made by individual wearers within local communities. The focus on the individual, existing as a part of a larger grouping, is important, reinforcing the potential for fashion as a tactic, which can be used by people in their everyday lives, as an agent for social change, rather than only as a commercial strategy by the fashion system. In short, the fashion discourse needed to change, and in the late twentieth and early twenty-first centuries there is evidence that it was doing so.

Ten years after the publication of my 2008 slow + fashion article, I contributed to a book by Turkish academic and designer Şölen Kipöz, which reflected the development of the wider slow + fashion discourse. In the intervening years there had been a considerable number of general and academic books and articles on fashion and sustainability. Nevertheless, the slow approach had not been advanced substantially for fashion and, as this book attests, still has the potential for greater development. Kipöz's *Slowness in Fashion* (2020), published in Turkish and English versions, proved timely. Ranging in content from consideration of emotionally durable fashion, through craft, economic models of slowing down fashion, design education, hedonic consumption, chronopolitics, upcycling, and international examples of practices, the book reiterates the ongoing significance and range of slow approaches to fashion. In his opening chapter, design activist, educator, and writer, Alastair Fuad-Luke shares his view that it was timely "to rethink Slowtopia in the age of instantaneity," citing Slow Food and Slow Cities as being pivotal to keeping the slow movement in the public eye.[11] He highlights the increasing use of the internet as a major shift for humanity, in connecting more people, speeding up communication, and offering increasingly visually compelling and competitive messages. Fuad-Luke reiterates his own earlier conceptualization of slow design (2002)[12] as a means of (re)balancing individual, social, and environmental well-being, and challenging the narrow anthropological perspective of global neoliberal economic models that define everyone as customers. He notes that designers could change this through activism and disruptive aesthetics. But the responsibility for change was wider, and must include wearers, who are complicit in how fashion is defined.

In 2017, British design historian and theorist Cheryl Buckley and I argued that definitions of "fashion" should not just be determined by the commodity-driven fashion system, but also valued as a means whereby people creatively explore, express, and embody identities, politics, and desires.[13] It was a perspective that had been enhanced by empirical investigation, such as by anthropologist Sophie Woodward in *Why Women Wear What They Wear* (2007).[14] This and other books highlighted the significance of ordinary items of clothing, as opposed to extraordinary styles, especially in women's wardrobes. The powerful relationships between women and their clothes were addressed for more general audiences by writers Sheila Heti, Heidi Julavitts, Leanne Shapton, and the "639 other" women of different ages, nationalities, and occupations who contributed stories as examples to their book *Women in Clothes* (2014). Similar publications helped to broaden an understanding of "fashion" beyond the market-driven definitions to acknowledge, amongst other things, the powerful material presence of fashion in everyday life in the form of garments that demand care and attention, recognition and understanding. At the same time, the implications of the increasing speed of fashion production and consumption were the subject of journalist Elizabeth Cline's *Overdressed: The Shockingly High Cost of Cheap Fashion* (2013), and the film *The True Cost* (2015).

Coincident with working on the chapter for Kipoz's book, I developed an article (2019) that explored some of the valuable contributions that were being made by women, which could inform a "slow + fashion" discourse and praxis[15] (presented first as a paper at an international conference, celebrating the tenth anniversary of the Centre for Sustainable Fashion at the London College of Fashion in October 2018). I drew attention to long-established beliefs and to clothing and textile methods that pre-dated and transcended modernity, and Eurocentricity. They were offered as ways of thinking, and as directions that had not been determined by the fashion system, capitalism, colonialism, or patriarchy. Such a shift in worldview could embrace everyday and indigenous practices and values, memory, sensory studies, micro-phenomenology, questions of authority and agency, equity, and social justice. They could lay the ground for slower fashion praxis.

This aligns with "small f" fashion, used as a verb, for the act of fashioning the body, contextualized relative to broader discourses of cultures, periods, and places, and respectful of planetary boundaries. The alternative, "big F" fashion, used as a noun, signifies the contemporary capitalist industry and system of power, originating in Europe, and exported throughout the world by Western imperialism. The former engages with fashion as *tactics*, as defined by thinker Michel de Certeau as a practice of resistance by ordinary people against imposed systems in their daily lives, to exhibit their agency as users and interpreters of culture.[16] Such actions have the capacity to challenge the strategic business models, commercial values, and resulting processes that underpin the "big F" fashion system. In my article I re-emphasize the power of the "+" between "slow" and "fashion," as a way of distinguishing a dynamic and revisionist project.

A similar perspective was endorsed early in the COVID-19 global pandemic by the astute professional forecaster Lidewij Edelkoort in her "World Hope Forum" Manifesto. She predicted changing patterns of behavior after the pandemic, declaring that "The comfort of being at and working from home, wasting time instead of money, has led people away from their addiction to material things and into a realm of sharing, caring and making." Plus, instant gratification from online shopping was stymied at the beginning of the pandemic, by the overloading of mail systems causing longer waits for the delivery of orders. Edelkoort described the virus as, "a representation of our conscience … it brings to light what is so terribly wrong with society and every day that becomes more clear … It teaches us to slow down and to change our ways."[17]

In order to explore how fashion might slow down, this book is organized into three main sections. The first section, "Speeding Up" presents fashion "as it is" today and how it got here, with an emphasis on the prevalence of "fast fashion." Section 2, "Slowing Down" looks at "where we have been" in respect of contexts and practices that foreground the emergence of slow approaches to fashion. While the need to reflect on *practices* is mentioned in the book, contemporary fashion tends to be defined by and through products, as is clear in Section 2. One of the challenges for a slow approach to fashion is to achieve a paradigm shift from product to practices, as is explored in Section 3 of the book. The third section, "Redirection," therefore considers the different forms of fashion and cultural understanding and practices needed for a future slow praxis for fashion. The book ends with a short "Call to Action," in the form of pithy provocations and reflections intended to stimulate individuals to act and react more slowly going forward.

It should be noted that the book focuses predominantly on contexts and examples from the Global North. This is not intended as an omission, or as an erasure of the enormous impact that the fashion system has in the Global South, not least on labor practices and on the creation of human and material waste. But this author is writing in and from a perspective formed largely in the Global North, which is also where many of the conditions, which need to be addressed in this book, originate. The slow lens revealed in the pages that follow is intended to provide an ethical and reflective challenge for fashion stakeholders, most notably wearers of clothes (that is, all of us), offering real possibilities for redefining dressing in more plural ways that reflect individual agency, preferences, and tastes.

1
SPEEDING UP

In March 2024, the online retailer Temu offered a pair of faux-fur boots for $0, which one commentator viewed as an indication that "fast fashion" had sunk to a new low.[1] Fast fashion was a sign of the times, with an emphasis on sign, rather than on the actual material product, which in this case appeared to be a close copy of a branded item. By the twenty-first century, fast fashion was ubiquitous, and fashion in general had entered the lives of more people around the globe, and in more complex ways. It equates with "the speed of communications; of transmissions; and even the speed with which human beings establish connections with one another."[2] "Big F" fashion expanded its reach through products, channels of communication, promotion, sales, and colonization, enabling greater numbers of people than ever before to participate in fashion as producers or consumers. Fast fashion brought more and cheaper clothes to more consumers, under a specious sense of "democratization."[3] However, the human cost was substantial for the many thousands of clothing factory workers, who were badly paid and subjected to unfavorable and dangerous conditions. Fast fashion produces exceptional amounts of human and material waste. It has also contributed to weakening the symbolic and emotional relationships between people and their clothes. The speed involved also reduces the opportunity for thought and reflection—thinking slowly, and then acting, can be a basis for rebellion. Slower approaches to fashion, discussed in detail in Section 2, emerged in response to the baser aspects of fast fashion, if not as its literal opposite. They aimed at counteracting some of the more exploitative and wasteful characteristics of the latter, as well as encouraging a greater appreciation of what we wear on our bodies. But first, this section begins with "where we are," by way of examining how fashion speeded up.

Fast Fashion

The standardization and mass production of clothes in the earlier twentieth century paved the way for the emergence of fast fashion by the end of the century. The latter developed from a product-driven concept based on a manufacturing model of "quick response" initiated in the United States in the 1980s. The Italian brand Benetton became a leader in developing rapid communication between its shops and factories, enabling shorter lead times for production, as well as a strong brand identity through its United Colors of Benetton marketing campaign. The globalized production and mass marketing of fashion resulted in cheaper garments, for more consumers, with retail and brand names being used increasingly to promote and sell products. In the following decade, branding was being described as a form of product differentiation or a "more reflexive capitalism" with its own discourse, which could be manipulated by companies. As conspicuous consumption reached a peak, labels became the symbols of aspirational status. Throughout the fashion sector, brand names came to serve as a means of "authenticating" a consumer's purchases and fashion sensibility and of displaying their fashion knowledge. In the mass market, fashion brands began to wield a wider economic and cultural influence, which was to develop significantly in the twenty-first century, with the greater global reach of fashion retailers. The Spanish label Zara was the first to become synonymous with "fast fashion," a term coined in *The New York Times* in December 1989, when the brand opened its initial store on Lexington Avenue in Manhattan. Defined by a strategy of reproducing designer looks for the mass market at relatively low prices, fast fashion became synonymous with rapid product turnover and cheaper clothes.

The number of fast fashion brands soon increased. In the United States for example, the commercial success of Zara was followed by Swedish H&M, Spanish Mango, Top Shop from the UK, the US Forever 21, and then other brands, such as the Irish Primark, Uniqlo from Japan, and later the Chinese e-commerce brand Shein. The established seasonal fashion cycles of about six months from design to consumer began to be replaced in the 1990s by much shorter timelines. In 2007, it was reported that Inditex, the parent company of Zara, had reduced their design-to-retail cycle to five weeks, rather than the standard five to six months. Styles were constantly updated in stores, and stock adjustments were made rapidly in response to sudden decreases or increases in fashion trends. Prices ranged from US$5.00 for knitted gloves, $27 for a mini skirt and $145 for a coat, with appropriately fake fur collar and cuffs.[4] The similarity in global reach, and to the speed and instant gratification offered by fast food, gained the fashion phenomenon the name "McFashion." Like fast food, fast fashion is mass-produced, standardized, and sold in ever-increasing quantities at low prices across a widening global market. Not only had fashion production changed, but in the process so had the very nature and definition of *fashion*.

Teri Agins, then a reporter for *The Wall Street Journal*, subtitled her 1999 book *The End of Fashion: How Marketing Changed the Clothing Business Forever*. In it she documented the rise of large-scale fashion brands in the 1990s, as a reflection of a homogenization of taste and consumer values. Fashion, she explained, was no longer put on a pedestal distinct from ordinary clothes, or primarily accessible to the socially and economically elite. Fast fashion brands had apparently, but questionably, served to democratize, enabling lower priced versions of the latest runway fashions to be available at a mass consumer level. In parallel, so-called "luxury" brands, led by French conglomerates such as LVMH (Louis Vuitton Moët Hennessy), formed in 1987, PPR (established in 1994, and later known as Kering), and Richemont, founded in 1988, were experiencing corporate takeovers and consolidations, towards greater shares of the fashion market.

More affordable products were being created, especially accessories and fragrances, which disseminated brand names and identities at price points available to more pockets. As a result, former distinctions between high end and high street fashion began to blur. A seminal moment came in 2004 when designer Karl Lagerfeld, head of the house of Chanel, collaborated with H&M. Quoted as saying "The future will only be about high and low. Everything else in between will disappear,"[5] Lagerfeld created thirty black and white pieces priced from €19.90 to €149.90 (US$25–$175). His was to be the first of a series of commercially very successful capsule collection collaborations between H&M and internationally famous designers and celebrities. When the first H&M location in the United States opened in April 2000 on New York's Fifth Avenue, *The New York Times* journalist, Ruth La Ferla, commended the retailer on its timing, observing that consumers had recently become more likely to hunt for bargains and dismiss department stores, since it was now "chic to pay less."[6] Fast fashion would become the retail success of the millennium, with other brands soon following suit, first on the high street and then, perhaps inevitably, online with retailers such as the UK-based ASOS, Chinese Shein, and then app-based Temu.

Production increased in regions offering low wages, to become more "cost effective" for businesses, retail prices dropped, and consumption grew. Fast fashion was not shaped literally by speed, but by a set of capitalist business practices focused on achieving continuous economic growth. As Kate Fletcher and others have pointed out, the logic of growth is well established in the fashion sector, as part of the world economy, which increased its size by a factor of five from the middle of the twentieth century. The expansion of fashion production (especially in Asia and the Global South), took place at a distance from many fashion wearers (in the Global North). As a result, fast fashion enabled and arguably relied on consumers to be largely disconnected from the reality of its "poverty wages, forced overtime, and climate change."[7] Economic goals lowered prices to encourage the more frequent purchase of fashion garments, in more places, resulting in clothing items being valued less by consumers, who discarded them more frequently, producing greater material waste (echoing the discards of the manufacturing process). After all, consumer society was not predicated on serving "need," but on encouraging "want," by making individuals feel deprived and incomplete unless they had access to the new and latest thing, or what was "in fashion." Many critics have agreed with Karl Marx, that contemporary consuming was an increasingly destructive concept, meant to devour or destroy, and pursued to fill up an internal sense of emptiness. Thus, the individual objects being consumed became of less significance than the act of consumption. Comparatively, it was a context completely distinct from the "modern gastronome," described by Carlo Petrini, founder of Slow Food, as someone with cultural awareness, an informed global perspective and capable of fine sensory analysis. The "fast life" was rooted in the contemporary world of globalization and the information society, facilitated by legislation, and faster production.

Fashion Production

The expiration of the Global Multi-Fibre Agreement (MFA) and General Agreement on Trade and Tariffs (GATT), on January 1, 2005, restricted the import of Chinese textiles and clothing to Europe, and had a significant impact on world clothing production.[8] Garment manufacturing in China and India increased as a result and developing countries such as Bangladesh and Cambodia entered global garment making. Although some interim production quotas remained in place, the new trading relationships were complex and difficult, leading to increased competition for European factories. In 2005, the European Union (EU) imposed new quotas on imports to protect textile industries in southern Europe from competition from lower-priced Chinese goods. As a result, retailers and wholesalers rushed to order supplies from China, causing textile firms to accelerate their exports to the EU, filling their quota for 2005. This caused the so-called "bra wars" that year, when 80 million Chinese-made garments were blocked at EU ports. The ban was lifted only when China agreed not to export any more trousers, sweaters, and bras that year, and to count half of the blocked items against its agreed 2006 annual quota. European and American factories were unable to compete with the cheaper prices and lower wages offered by Asian producers, thus changing the map of world clothing production, and decreasing the anticipated retail prices of fashionable garments.

From 2000 to 2007, clothing exports from China increased annually by 18 percent into the United States and 21 percent into the EU, and the amount of items purchased escalated incrementally. Global clothing production doubled in the first fifteen years of the twenty-first century, driven by a growing middle-class population worldwide and increased per capita sales in mature economies. The main agent was fast fashion with its quicker turnaround of new styles, more collections being produced annually, and at cheaper prices. Despite the economic advantages for manufacturers and brands, the popularity of fast fashion brought huge, and negative, environmental and human impact. Even though some fashion businesses began to respond to environmental concerns, the effect was bound to be limited, because the creation, production and wearing of fashion happened across vast distances. Added to which, different steps in the garment production processes occurred in different countries, creating potential missteps between operations. As competitive economic advantage in manufacturing and labor costs moved to developing countries, textile and clothing production shifted also. In 2006, around 7 percent of all world clothing exports were reported as being manufactured by 26.5 million, mainly women, workers, many of whom were paid below living wages, and labored in sweatshop conditions. By 2020, China dominated the market, exporting US$109.9 billion worth of textiles and $158.4 billion worth of clothing each year. In the process, corporatization imposed an instrumental view of time and people, reflected in the lower wages and conditions of workers. An undercover report in 2022 on fast fashion e-commerce brand Shein revealed that workers at one of its factories were paid a base salary of 4,000 yuan per month, the equivalent of roughly US$556, to make at least 500 pieces of clothing per day. Many toiled for long hours to earn a commission of 0.14 yuan, or two cents, per item.[9] Such conditions were not untypical, but were being ignored for a combination of reasons, including a lack of political will to acknowledge them and the fear of withdrawal of funds by foreign investors. The circumstances of clothing manufacture remained largely anonymous to global consumers and even to brands themselves, who worked through local subcontractors. It took a tragedy to bring wide attention to working conditions.

In April 2013, the terrible consequences of the distanced and disconnected global production of fashion came to international attention with the collapse of the Rana Plaza clothing factory in Savar, an industrial suburb of Dhaka, Bangladesh. The deadliest disaster in the history of garment production (although not the only recent one), it killed 1,134 people and injured 2,500 others, mainly women. It served to focus global attention on the unsafe conditions in the garment industry in Bangladesh, by then the world's second-leading exporter of clothing, behind China. Offering amongst the lowest wages in the world to garment workers, the country's more than 5,000 clothing factories produced for a wide spectrum of the world's fashion brands and retailers, including UK fast fashion brand Primark, U.S. Walmart, and Italian luxury brands Gucci and Prada. The tragedy resulted in wider improvements in factory safety being initiated by Western brands, fearful of losing consumers, working with local unions and the Bangladeshi government. Included was giving greater transparency to the supply chain, a call for local monitoring of safety standards within Bangladesh, and a recognition of how, in so many ways, cheap clothes were not cheap, certainly not when the consequence could be the loss of human lives. Ten years later, buildings had been made safer, but more holistic protection for workers was weak. Only 27 percent of the 7,000 garment factories in Bangladesh participated in a major international standards initiative created to protect workers following

Rana Plaza's collapse, leaving an estimated three million workers without protection.[10] The tragedy instituted action in the supply chain, as businesses, governments, and consumers demanded transparency of working conditions, factories, and the processes behind products, but actual legislation did not follow. Fast fashion and "just in time" manufacturing continued to exert tremendous downwards pressure on wages and costs, resulting in suppliers continuing to cut corners. (At the time of writing, in 2024, new laws are being planned to mandate greater environmental, social, and governance (ESG) disclosures, documentation, and tracking. Planned legislation, such as New York's Fashion Sustainability and Social Accountability Act, and the European Climate Law, and European Union Corporate Sustainability Reporting Directive are expected to require chain-of-custody reporting and supply chain mapping. Companies failing to comply will face heavy penalties and fines.)

Fast/er Fashion Practices

The Rana Plaza disaster emphasized the consequences of the physical distance between fashion production and consumption. The process whereby clothes come into existence was anonymized, and an implicit disconnect existed between where items were produced and where they *became fashion*, through promotion, branding, and advertising. By contrast, high-end fashion brands including Burberry, Tom Ford, Moschino, and Versace (Versus) began giving the public access to, once exclusive, fashion shows. Viewers were enabled to "see now, buy now," directly from the catwalk, mimicking the rapid turnaround of fast fashion. An increase in online shopping also altered the relationship of consumers with garments. More and more, clothes were purchased almost entirely based on how they looked, with purchasers knowing little of how and where garments were made or about their materials.

Observing a generational shift, Teri Agins commented how Generation Xers, born in the 1970s, had been brought up to dress casually and were unable "to discern quality in clothes."[11] The decline in Europe and North America of the teaching of Home Economics in schools, and more women undertaking paid work outside of the home, had diminished knowledge of how to mend clothes, and reduced the time allocated to making and repairing. Added to which, the synthetic fabrics characteristic of fast fashion were not produced primarily with the intention of being mended.

The greater use of central heating and air conditioning in the twentieth century meant that for many people a need to gain material protection from their clothes had become less significant than in former times, enabling garments to be chosen more based on their appearance rather than their use value. A focus on the *look* increased in the twenty-first century with the growth of social media and online shopping, with purchases being based only on sight, not on touch or fit. Fashion had become a spectacle with "*capital* accumulated to the point that it become[s] images," as foreseen by Marxist French philosopher Guy Debord in the 1960s.[12] Debord highlighted the power and agency of images in modern production and commodity-based societies, and how the social and sensory relationship between people and fashion was increasingly mediated by still and moving impressions. The extent and rapidity of engagement with images in everyday life impacted the contemporary sensory relationship of the wearer to the actual fashion garment. But while images can literally appear and disappear in the virtual world, physical clothes do not have the same transient property.

Shifts were happening in the Global North as to where many people bought their clothes, resulting in fewer fashion purchases being made from conventional "brick and mortar" stores. In the United States, the UK, and Europe, more supermarkets and big box stores offered "value fashion," retailed alongside food and household items, giving clothes an equivalence to other ordinary and everyday consumables. The result was not just that clothing was purchased more cheaply in these outlets, but that items were bought more frequently, with less time given to think about what was being bought, and many more items being available. Evidence of speed in fashion shopping was testified with the opening of Primark on London's Oxford Street, in Spring 2007, when 3,000 customers stampeded into the shop. The very act of consuming fashion had speeded up. Fast fashion brands gained popular appeal based on low prices, but also on a rapid turnover of styles, rather than on quality, spurred on by brands such as Zara and H&M, or Top Shop, Primark, and Matalan, as well as Forever 21 in the United States. The Japanese giant Uniqlo achieved huge global expansion by incorporating more basic clothing items, like underwear, and innovative fabrics, rather than relying only on rapidly changing fashion-focused styles.

From a material perspective, fast fashion has been referred to as "fossil fashion," as more garments are made of synthetic fibers, in particular polyester, or of fiber blends.[13] It continues a major shift that began early in the twentieth century, when synthetics became more widely available. Nylon, launched in the late 1930s, was followed later by acrylic and polyester, all lauded for their "wash and wear" qualities. Being quick to launder, and wrinkle free, these fabrics diminished the need for ironing. By the late 1960s, the production of synthetics exceeded natural fibers, and polyester was emerging as the most popular inexpensive fabric.[14] In the process, no significant attention was given to the lengthy degradation of synthetic fabrics, or to the fact that they shed microfibers, which are known to have proved harmful to people and nature. By 2019, polyester accounted for over 50 percent of world fiber production. In the same year the first world Plastic Health Summit examined the effects of plastic on well-being. New textile technology was promoted as beneficial. Toray, the fine polyester fabric developed for Uniqlo's AIRism line, for example, was effective in its claims to wick away perspiration quickly, be breathable, and provide a smooth and cool feel to the body. Polyester became a mainstay for fast fashion, due in part to its quick and easy-care properties. Like nylon, it is partly derived from petroleum, is energy intensive to produce, and in the process emits nitrous oxide, or "greenhouse gas." Added to which, not only do polyester fabrics emit microfibers, but they can take from 20 to 200 years to decompose, meaning that garments do not just endure fashion's faster cycles, but can also outlive wearers, often by decades. Influenced by fast fashion, and by more frequent changes of styles, consumers were being encouraged to consider fashionable clothing as disposable. But gradually, any sense that this was a "a good thing" began to diminish. The attitude of "more" had become instilled into the growth-based mandate of fashion brands, with increasing consequences.

Patterns of fashion consumption expanded worldwide in the twenty-first century, especially in Europe, the United States, and Australia. But with increased consumption of cheaper clothes came more frequent disposal, and the resultant creation of more waste. According to U.S. Environmental Protection Agency estimates, in 2016, Americans were throwing away about 12.8 million tons of textiles annually, or the equivalent of 80 pounds for each man, woman, and child. In 2023, UK consumers were reported as buying more clothes per person than any other country in Europe, from an industry worth £32 billion. But four out of five people owned at least some clothes that remained unworn because they no longer fitted or they needed altering, and around 30 percent of clothing in wardrobes had not been worn for at least a year. In Australia, clothing is the fastest-growing household waste, with Australians dumping 6000kg of clothing and textile waste into landfill every ten minutes in 2022.[15] The huge expansion of fashion consumption in China, first with the popularity of foreign brands and then with an increase of Chinese labels, added substantially to global textile waste. In 2022, China was reported as having produced roughly 22 million tonnes (metric tons) of textile waste, with only 1.5 million tonnes, or about 20 percent of the total, being recycled.

Wearers and brands were all culpable in engendering a wider culture of waste for fashion. In 2010, a major H&M store in midtown Manhattan was challenged by *The New York Times* for destroying unsold stock before disposing of it, making it unwearable. It was a practice not only found in the fast fashion sector. Luxury clothing conglomerates Richemont and Louis Vuitton were called out, as was Burberry, for burning £28.6 million worth of unsold products in 2017, to retain its "brand value." Criticism from environmental campaigners, and in the press, curtailed the practice. Vast quantities of clothing and textile waste was also being produced at the consumer level. The procedure could be to the detriment of local economies, especially in the Global South, and to places that wanted to start their own fashion industries. Images of Kantamanto Market in Accra, Ghana, the largest used clothing market in West Africa, circulated widely, showing mountains of used and unsold new clothing shipped mainly from the UK, North America, and Europe. The waste has come to be known as *Dead White Men's Clothes*, also the title of a 2021 Australian documentary on the subject, named to signal the local assumption about many of the unworn items. On a more positive note, this clothing distribution has provided income for a complex ecosystem of independent traders, who sell, recreate, and reconstruct the imported clothes; 25 million garments a month are repaired and upcycled by local entrepreneurs, enabling the location to function as "a lab, a factory, a studio, a community center and a market all in one."[16] However, about 40 percent or at least 1 million pounds of the clothing is typically in poor condition and eventually ends up in landfills or informal dumping sites.

As Brooks, Fletcher et al. have pointed out, used clothing does not just "go away," it goes "somewhere."[17] Kantamanto's secondhand clothing dealers have lobbied, so far unsuccessfully, for legislation to stop the practice of exporting waste items, which has been informed by a colonial-based mindset. When the motivation is *having* more fashionable clothes, consideration of where they come from or will go to cannot compete with the powerful lure presented by the fashion image. Yet the gratification promised by fashion advertising will always prove short-lived and can never guarantee fulfillment. If a relationship is not formed between person and object, the latter is more likely to be discarded, especially when its fashion value wanes, even if its use value remains.

Clothes and accessories that go out of fashion are destined to be discarded as trash, and assigned to landfills, often located in places as far removed from consumers as the sites of production are. Any form of *sustainable* fashion must therefore be acknowledged as a social practice beyond consumerism, as Otto von Busch has indicated in response to the question, "What is to be sustained?"[18]

Academic Andrew Brooks has asked what compels people (in the Global North) to purchase more and more clothes? Brooks concluded that the "compulsion" to buy was a result of being manipulated by fast fashion brands that priced garments artificially low to increase sales. The arrival of online fashion retailers such as ASOS (founded in London in 2000), Boohoo (in UK, 2019), and Shein (in China, 2008), or Temu (China, 2015), added to what was available, and focused on instant gratification. Many lower-priced garments were promoted as "budget" versions of more expensive designs (or "dupes," as Gen Z would say). For instance, Fashion Nova, a popular Instagram brand, was praised by *Cosmopolitan* for recreating Meghan Markle's Stella McCartney evening wedding dress for the "dirt cheap" price of US$44.99.[19] It was evident that a system had developed that writer Aja Barber describes as perpetuating "urgency, detachment, and indifference toward clothing," and being harmful, "to culture, ethos, and ways of life."[20]

Fast fashion not only promoted low prices, but for some it even offered the lure of becoming celebrities of sorts through fashion practices, which did not necessarily involve wear. One of the more bizarre examples of disconnection from garments has been the "shopping haul," an online trend that started about 2008, and took advantage of the growing impact of YouTube, and later of TikTok. Shopping haul videos, typically made at home by young women, featured clothes, cosmetics, and household items purchased entirely for the purpose of display and showing off. Products were usually selected for their appearance, their fashion currency, and their low cost. Beginning during the global recession period, the videos provided a voyeuristic thrill by showing how disposable incomes could be spent, or envied. For the "haulers" the appeal was the possibility of becoming famous, based on their number of viewers, and the hope that brands might sponsor them, with goods or income, to promote their products. But the practice also reinforced fashion as being highly visual, not material, as disposable, and an altogether "quick fix" in terms of its accessibility and facility for gratification. People (especially young women) were buying (cheap) clothes because they liked the look of them, usually when seen on the bodies of other people. Many "hauled" items would be shared and then returned to the store or online source from which they came or simply be cast aside. As the #haul trend became a social media marketing tool for fashion brands to gain more customers, the quality of what was purchased declined. (Amazon has since introduced "Haul," an exclusively mobile phone facility, which ships directly from the manufacturer to the consumer, where items take longer to arrive than other online brands like Shein or Temu, but cutting prices to under $20 per article.)

The haul practice was evidence of how the popular discourse of fashion was influenced by a progressively diverse and rapid flow of media. As celebrities were adopted as fashion icons, ordinary people aspired to a similar status, enhanced around the start of the millennium with the appearance of the "fashion influencer," who was established by 2010. The most successful influencers, who were paid money or in products, became fashion gatekeepers, whose opinions really *mattered* to consumers. Celebrities increasingly took on these roles in the twenty-first century, and while they could have been extremely powerful in advocating for a more ethical, caring, less wasteful, and less greedy fashion system, few did. One notable exception is actress Angelina Jolie.[21] But as a UK *Guardian* article noted, so-called "greenwashing influencers" gained in popularity. The employment in 2021 of "famous for being famous" celebrity Kourtney Kardashian as "sustainability ambassador" by fast fashion retailer Boohoo was but one example of "halfhearted eco initiatives" by a brand. "Eco-adjacent influencing" was also extremely common, where a celebrity espoused ethical practices, while at the same time promoting a fast fashion brand for a fee. Because influencing demanded constantly maintaining audience attention, it aligned very well with the objectives of fast fashion. Both are fundamentally antithetical to true sustainability, which demands "slowing down and being satisfied with what we have and only [buying] what we need."[22] Unfortunately, the fashion system is predicated on *want* not on *need.* As a result, the rethinking of the very nature and definition of *fashion*, informed by slower principles, had to happen through new channels.

Fashion / Praxis

Concerns over faster fashion practices came to wider attention in the twenty-first century, and not only in the press. Around the globe, the number of exhibitions devoted to fashion gained increasing popularity and also offered a platform for reflection and critique. Three examples are offered here, the first being *Fast Fashion: The Dark Sides of Fashion,* held at the Museum Europäischer Kulturen, in Berlin, from late 2019 to early 2021, conceived by the Museum für Kunst und Gewerbe in Hamburg. The exhibition revealed how the greatest "fashion sins" were committed before garments reached stores. The production of a single cotton T-shirt, for example, consumed 2,700 liters of water, which regularly ended up spreading the toxic pollutants used in chemical dyeing processes into rivers. As a result, people living in fashion manufacturing hubs such as Bangladesh suffered from persistent environmental pollution and contaminated groundwater. The show emphasized the concerns of increasing numbers of consumers about the working conditions and wages of largely female workforces of seamstresses in the global clothing industry. Explaining how fast fashion functioned and how producers and consumers were interconnected, it encouraged visitors to rethink the impact for the environment of what they bought, and to get involved in dealing with the effect. A section focusing on "slow fashion" was informed by Neonyt, an annual sustainable fashion fair held in Berlin. Audio interviews were available, recording "slow and sustainable pioneers," such as Jenna Stein, an organizer of clothing swap parties. Slow approaches were not only part of this exhibition, or specific to Germany, they were evident also in other countries.

In 2020, Leeds Museums and Galleries in the North of England put fashion consumption in a wider historical context. *Fast x Slow Fashion: Shopping for Clothes in Leeds 1720–2020* highlighted ways that people had been fashionable in the past, and not only by buying new clothes. In emphasizing how handmade, recycled, and pre-owned fashion had made a resurgence in an age of Climate Change Action, this exhibition also explained the significant legacy of textile production and trade in Leeds. Gaining an understanding of local history and its intersection with global conditions was an important part of this and other initiatives that aimed to encourage people to stop, think, and then act. *Fast Fashion/Slow Art,* at the Corcoran School of the Arts and Design Gallery, Washington DC, in 2019, had a different conceptual framework, but the message was the same. Reminding visitors of the prodigious outsourcing of production in the United States, where 97 percent of clothing sold was produced in nations deemed to be "developing," conscientious consumers were urged to take agency in order to change the path of fast fashion. Appropriate actions were shared, including checking the tags when buying new clothing, trying to avoid synthetic petroleum-based fibers (rayon, nylon, polyester, acrylic, and spandex), buying secondhand, supporting makers who used clean supply chains, mending what was broken, and learning how to repurpose items. Demonstrating their message by featuring local creators, cultures, histories, and potential action by wearers through practices such as clothing swaps, these exhibitions reinforced the possibilities of slow praxis for fashion, which will be discussed in more detail in the next section.

2 SLOWING DOWN

To seek the origins of slow praxis for fashion we must look to the contextual changes which occurred in the 1980s and 1990s, encapsulated by the foundation of the Slow Food Movement, as well as to alterations in the fashion system, notably the arrival of fast fashion. There was an awakening sense of responsibility towards the environment occurring during that period. In reaction, Ezio Manzini hypothesized about moving away from product-based well-being, to valuing community assets more highly, as "islands of slowness" that encouraged more individual participation in everyday life.[1] We can apply the concept to fashion. The speed associated with modernity and fossil-powered progress, and the assumption that higher speeds were always better than lower ones, needed to be challenged, to make space for what Manzini and collaborator François Jégou refer to as "contemplative time." They agreed simply, but powerfully, that it is unlikely that a society that moves in the fast lane can ever be environmentally sustainable. The value of care and slowness were identified as the expression of an emerging cultural attitude that respects looking after items and taking time to do things properly to achieve high standards in life. It is of no coincidence that a movement such as Slow Food, which has made the word *slow* the very emblem of its strategy, gained traction in more frenetic societies such as the United States or Japan. Nor is it by chance that writers, economists, town planners, designers, sociologists, and philosophers increasingly addressed the topic of slowness in the late twentieth century.

Design writer and thinker John Thackara proposed "selective slowness," to embrace a greater variety of speeds in life to achieve a sense of balance, which is determined by individuals, not by systems that we cannot control.[2] The concept can be applied directly to fashion, as being defined both personally by what individuals choose to wear, and as an external system which effectively dictates what is available. Attitudes to time underlie how we relate, or not, to the concept of slow, as well as determining what is, or is not, "in fashion." Fashion has been described as embodying the notion of time more than many phenomena. Rooted in the "latest," fashion creates its own past through rapidly changing styles, always on the verge of becoming something else, and in that sense it speculates about the future. A *slow* praxis for fashion, by contrast, can be more aligned to American architect Bruce Goff's notion of the "continuous present," a term borrowed from writer Gertrude Stein. It is a valuable concept that references how we experience time, and how we can only dress in the *present*, releasing us from the sense of a *fashion* time, which is always aiming at the future. It equates with Stewart Brand's definition of the *now* as,

> the period in which people feel they live and act and have responsibility. For most of us now that is a week, sometimes a year. For some traditional tribes in the American northeast and Australia *now* is seven generations back and forward (175 years in each direction).[3]

Parkins and Craig reinforce the need for a shift in temporal mindset: "To declare the value of slowness … is to promote a position counter to the dominant value-system of 'the times'."[4] The statement is germane to this section of the book, which considers "where we have been," first in respect of the developing interest in environmentalism that predated *slow* approaches, and then for fashion.

Environmentalism—Redesigning Terms and Values

The foundation of the environmentalist movement is attributed to the publication of *Silent Spring* (1962) by marine biologist and conservationist, Rachel Carson. She warned of the dangers to the natural environment of chemical pesticides, such as DDT, endangering also animals and humans, for economic gain. The book foregrounded the struggle to identify and then to name the changes needed to achieve a more ethical and sustainable quality of life. From the 1970s, it had a foundational impact on approaches to design, in Europe and the United States. Terms evolved such as "alternative design" and "design for need" that gave way to catchphrases like "eco-design," "green design," and then in the 1980s and 1990s, to "environmentally affirmative design."[5] "Eco-" came to serve as a convenient prefix for anything to do with environmental issues, including fashion. In the late 1980s, John Button included three pages of "eco-" terms in his *A Dictionary of Green Ideas* (1988). Writing in the mid-1970s, environmentalist and academic Tim O'Riordan viewed this more eco-focused language as evidence of how the "environmental perspective" had become deeply embedded in the social and political fabric.[6] Design historian Pauline Madge shared the view that environmental concerns had come to penetrate daily lives and influence "our judgements, our moral positions, our systems of belief, and our everyday conduct."[7] Changes in language, then and now, reveal underlying shifts in social and political attitudes. *Slow* can be viewed as a continuation of this semantic struggle, albeit one that took its own form and direction, distinct from the wider governmental and legislative strategies of the 1970s and 1980s. Madge noted how the 1972 "Only One Earth" United Nations (UN) conference provided context for the first wave of alternative technology. Preceding the OPEC (Organization of the Petroleum Exporting Countries) oil embargo of 1973, and the 1974 oil crisis, the conference signaled the start of environmental action and the identification of "design for need."[8] But while well-intended, this paradigm shift caused scant long-term change to professional design and had no direct impact on fashion design.

"Green" became a popular term, frequently used euphemistically. John Button dated its origins to the late 1970s. For many, it was associated with the international direct action campaigning group, Greenpeace, founded in Canada in 1971. The political activities of The Green Party in the UK in the early 1980s also gave "green" an equivalence to "environmental," and enhanced its political edge. The "Greens" came to refer to supporters of leftwing Green politics, especially in West Germany. In the *Friends of the Earth Handbook* (1987), Jonathan Porritt, a prominent UK Green party member, further distinguished between "light greens" (reformers or realists) and "dark greens" (radicals). For some, Green symbolized a "new spring when all things start afresh."[9] Button also noted how the Greens wore casual clothes, thus distinguishing members collectively, and setting them apart from the more establishment looks of besuited politicians. Their sartorial impact was unremarkable otherwise. However, it highlights how much of this activity was product directed rather than being aimed at consumers, or at changing systems or processes. While many design professionals responded positively to the phenomenon of "green design," their activities were conceived within the capitalist status quo and built on consumerism.

Design for want (not need) and market-driven priorities was impacted by overarching neoliberal attitudes. In the 1980s, the British government endorsed its Design Council's adoption of the slogan "good design is good business." The catchphrase, originating in the United States in the 1970s with the IBM Corporation, championed the sleekness of modern design, and the slickness of corporate culture. It is perhaps of little surprise therefore that "green design" was interpreted through green consumerism, as part of "The New Green Society," legitimized in Britain by Conservative Prime Minister Margaret Thatcher in the late 1980s. Likewise, in the United States, Republican President Ronald Reagan reinforced neoliberal agendas that encouraged the deregulation of economies, privatization, and free-market capitalism. It spurred the decline of manufacturing and the rise of the service sector, with new brands emerging in the 1980s as corporate assets. The areas of retail design, packaging, exhibition design, and fashion, all embraced a "green approach" to design, which John Button described as eclectic, drawing ideas from a wide range of disciplines. By the end of the 1980s, green design, green capitalism, and green consumerism were being connected and referred to in numerous publications. The best-selling *Green Consumer Guide* (1989) by British environmentalist John Elkington targeted what the individual consumer could do to save the environment. *The Ethical Consumer*, a UK-based non-profit bi-monthly magazine, and the *New Consumer* both sought a shift in corporate behavior toward a future that was more sustainable, economically, socially, and environmentally. But, as design critic Nigel Whiteley noted, in "high-consumption, marketing orientated, capitalist society, the 'Green consumer' was—almost invariably—first and foremost a consumer, and only nominally Green."[10] Green design was essentially at odds with prevailing twentieth-century modernist design logic. The latter reflected a commitment to simplifying and standardizing products, and the "logic of mass-production processes … reason over emotion, order over chaos, and even the triumph of man's will over nature."[11] Such marketing-driven strategies are the antithesis of the slow approach being put forward in this book.

Environmental issues came to wider attention with the publication, in 1987, of *Our Common Future*, the Brundtland Report, by the World Commission on Environment and Development (WCED) convened by the United Nations. It established a concise, and still prevailing, definition of sustainable development, "that meets the needs of the present without compromising the ability of future generations to meet their own needs."[12] The report advocated eco-efficient growth fueled by technological innovation. This has subsequently been described as a "Promethean" approach, which contrasts with the slower "Soterean" advocacy that separates fashion from the unsustainable growth promoted by capitalism.[13] While "sustainability" became a more acceptable term than "eco," it was a strategy predicated on growth, expansion, and GDP (Gross Domestic Product), reflective of Abraham Maslow's famed hierarchy of needs. Established in the 1940s, Maslow proclaimed the goal of self-actualization was based on material wealth. A slow approach, by contrast, is more attuned to psychologist Erich Fromm's warning in 1976, that the elevation in affluent societies of *having* far above *being* had resulted in a disastrous imbalance. Non-sustainable patterns of consumption and production in the Global North was contrasted with enormous poverty in the Global South.[14] But the Brundtland report was *somewhat slower* in its understanding that greater consumption was not a sustainable solution.

Brundtland laid the foundations for the Earth Summit, held in Rio de Janeiro in 1992, which led to the creation of the UN Commission on Sustainable Development. Then the Kyoto Protocol was signed in 1997, as an addendum to the UN Framework Convention on Climate Change (UNFCCC), to reduce greenhouse gas emissions, based on the scientific consensus that global warming was a reality, driven by human-made CO_2. Its recommendations eventually came into force in 2005, and it currently has ratification by 198 countries, (although it remains significantly lacking the consistent support of the United States). While a consolidated global approach was essential, responses to ethical issues varied in different countries, putting the responsibility on the individual rather than on corporations. The editors of *The Ethical Consumer* argued convincingly that green consumerism had failed "to lift the veil of brand-name products," and had thus perpetuated ignorance among consumers. Nigel Whiteley emphasized this point in his 1992 book with an image, from The Media Foundation of Canada, depicting a man with his mouth stuffed full of U.S. dollars, parodying a United Colors of Benetton advertisement with the tagline "The True Colors of Benetton."[15] The author defined such critique and boycotting of companies in the 1990s, as representing "ethical," as opposed to "green" consuming. Others, who perpetuated opinions counter to the prevailing (capitalist) value systems provided more solid foundations for the development of slow praxis.

Victor Papanek, a leading spokesperson on design and sustainability, vehemently challenged consumption-based strategies, founded in neoliberal attitudes, as having fostered "the greedy 1980s."[16] His *Design for the Real World* (1973) proved to be a seminal design text (although it did not refer to clothing). Still writing on the topic twenty years later, Papanek continued to caution,

> There can be little doubt that the environment and the ecological balance of the planet are no longer sustainable. Unless we learn to preserve and conserve Earth's resources, and change our most basic patterns of consumption, manufacture and recycling, we may have no future.[17]

These assumptions that many everyday things would only be used once or a few times, had marked an undesirable shift in consumer practices, values and attitudes to property.

American futurist Alvin Toffler cautioned in 1970 that the spread of disposable items would decrease the durability of the relationship between humans and man-made things. Where a single object might previously have been kept and valued over a relatively long period of time, connections were being made with more products and for shorter periods.[18] The epithet the Throwaway Society, coined originally in 1928 to refer to consumer culture in the United States, could increasingly be applied to the wider Western world. It was especially evident in fashionable clothes; we might think of the 1960s fad for paper dresses, which were intended to be disposable, but not biodegradable.

Toffler's influential book, *Future Shock* (1970), was prescient. It distinguished three stages of development in society and production: the agrarian, the industrial, and the post-industrial. The features of post-industrial society included the greater presence of disposable goods, and the rise in the cost of manual repair and cleaning. Toffler predicted that this scenario would lead to the rental of almost everything (from a ladder to a wedding dress), thus eliminating the need for ownership. Today, rental is still in embryo for fashion, but the practice has been lauded for promoting a circular economy, along with resale, repair, and other forms of durability (although renting, can be critiqued for the energy used in cleaning items between wear, and in transporting clothes between companies and wearers). But, more fundamentally, it is disposable *attitudes* to consumer goods that must be questioned, as influenced by a desire to be *in fashion*. Post-industrial society, as characterized by Toffler, had a sense of the temporary, be it about goods or human relationships. It foregrounded the twenty-first-century Information Age, the time of the computer, automation, distracted attention, ephemerality, and greater importance being attached to services.

Toffler's title reflected the psychological state of individuals and societies who perceive that they are experiencing too much change in too short a time. The impending millennium brought a sense of anticipation for some, and a sense of anxiety and even dread for others. Papanek's solution was to live more simply, or we could say slower, without quantities of possessions. Taking his role models from beyond modern Western societies, he cited the Inuit people as skillful designers, whose work he considered excellent because of their close relationships to climate, environment, space, and culture. He recommended concepts such as "sharing not buying," and twisted the modernist "form follows function" tagline into "form follows fun." His perspective on design was informed by human needs and well-being, not by growth, economic profit, and the acquisition of greater wealth. Papanek envisioned design as a political tool, aligned with the wider perspectives of the 1960s' and 1970s' counterculture, whose initiatives challenged a capitalist-driven status quo. His work remains a valuable point of reference for the development of slow praxis for fashion. It is also notable that his viewpoints were based on the empirical study of conceptual and spiritual ideas, and practices evident outside of modern Western consumer society.

Similarly, in his 1966 essay "Buddhist Economics," later included in his well-known collection *Small is Beautiful: A Study of Economics As If People Mattered* (1973), the economist E.F. Schumacher challenged the assumption underpinning capitalist-driven economics. He disagreed, in other words, that people who consumed more were better off than those who consumed less. It is an assessment that resonates with slow ways of thinking. Specifically,

> if the purpose of clothing is a certain amount of temperature comfort and an attractive appearance, the task is to attain this purpose with the smallest possible effort, that is, with the smallest annual destruction of cloth and with the help of designs that involve the smallest possible input of toil.[19]

Schumacher lauded garments made by the skillful draping of uncut cloth, over those employing complicated tailoring. He criticized material that was made to wear out quickly, and it being the height of barbarity to make anything ugly, shabby, or mean. His ideas were informed by Buddhist economics, where production from local resources for local needs was determined to be the most rational way of life. Contemporary with Schumacher's writing was the publication of *The Whole Earth Catalog,* an original magazine/catalog founded, edited, and published by Stewart Brand, between 1968 and 1972, and then sporadically until 1998. It celebrated amateurs, and focused on self-sufficiency, ecology, and alternative education, that is on imparting ideas, not on selling goods. Drawing on the philosophy of architect Buckminster Fuller, Brand saw the catalogs as a connective system and a tool for empowerment. In retrospect, such strategies can serve as ideologically foundational to slow thinking.

Fashion—Changes—More Slowly

In the fashion system, just as the terms "eco," "green," and "organic," were applied loosely for marketing purposes, as social and cultural interests transformed, "sustainable fashion" also came to be used interchangeably with the other terms. By definition, "sustainability" focuses on the environment and human life, and on "the capacity of a system or object to produce something desired over an extended period."[20] But (somewhat like the word "fashion") the term has been used indiscriminately and emptied of any real significance.

John Ehrenfeld reiterated how the fashion industry must embrace a meaningful definition of and goals for sustainability. But when that fashion system was conceptually defined by constant change, and spurred by the need for growth and economic profit, sustainability became an oxymoron—highly problematic to achieve, or even to conceive. The realization of more sustainable strategies in fashion could not be based only on what people *bought* but on how they *practiced* fashion. A slow model for fashion must unite ways of thinking and behaving (praxis), underpinned by new and potentially sustainable economies, and ideas of well-being that incorporate consideration of the time involved to produce, appreciate, and cultivate quality.

These were factors that were arguably at odds with the growth-dependent goals of the fashion system. But we must not forget that by the late twentieth century, *fashion* could not be defined in the singular, as being only one particular look for one time and one type of person.

Writing in 1989, for example, Angela McRobbie noted how practices of buying and wearing secondhand clothes in Britain had become so ubiquitous as to be "reinscribed into the fashion system."[21] They were significant in displaying the creativity and style of young people at a time of recession. An investigation of youth culture in Britain, Europe, North America, and beyond from the 1950s and 1960s provides further evidence of fashion being made by young people, literally and through their style management. Even if bought directly "off the rack," clothing items could be modified, and instilled with new meanings. We can think, most obviously, of the (continuing) impact of Hip Hop or Punk. The point being that, despite the increase in the number of fashion products available, by the late twentieth century more people were making fashion decisions, reflective of their beliefs, politics, identities, and their wallets, which could be counter to prevailing market-driven trends. Fashion's relationship to time, referred to already, also became more nuanced, moving away from the linear and chronological marking of time associated with modernity. By the 1980s, fashion designers who are now considered conceptual or avant-garde had begun to experiment with a different concept of time, closer to *kairos*, the Greek word associated with more qualitative, or what we might describe as *slower* time. While the examples which follow have not been read through a slow lens previously, doing so provides us with valuable possibilities for the implementation of slow praxis for fashion. They can be characterized by their "disruptive aesthetics" (based on a concept developed by French philosopher Jacques Rancière), allied to a sense of the "continuous present," referred to at the beginning of this section of the book, as well as to their strong material sensibility. These are characteristics that were especially evident in the work of Japanese designers Issey Miyake, Rei Kawakubo, and Yohji Yamamoto, who started to practice at the end of the 1970s.

Disruptive Aesthetics

In the early 1970s, Yohji Yamamoto pre-washed most of the clothes he offered for sale to remove a sense of "newness" from the garments. Rei Kawakubo famously introduced irregularities into the production of her "lace" knitwear sweaters, to create the sense of imperfection inherent to clothes made by hand. In doing so she brought the idea of patina and ageing to Paris fashion. It recalled the Japanese tradition of *boro boro*, where ragged and tattered pieces of cloth are mended or patched together (a technique that has also been explored, for example, by Reiko Sudo and her contemporary Japanese textile company, NUNO Corporation). This tactic, which challenges the uniformity associated with contemporary mass-produced fashion, can be read as *slow* (in retrospect, at least), and as the antithesis of striving for perfection in an industrial age. Also thinking slowly, Issey Miyake was the first designer to present a permanent, unchanging line, alongside his seasonal collections. He pioneered garments which could be worn more than one way, providing agency and flexibility to the wearer. Rei Kawakubo and Yohji Yamamoto both favored black and dark blue fabric from the early 1980s, earning them the name *karasu-zoku,* the crow tribe. It was a tactic that demanded perfect cut and volume, and enabled pieces to be worn together without a clashing of colors, aligned also to a bohemian rejection of more mainstream ideas about fashion.[22] Garments were cut loosely and layered, creating space around the body, as in Japanese dressing traditions, rather than being fitted to it, as has been the norm in the West. Speaking in his 1993 film about Yamamoto, director Wim Wenders observed how,

> Yamamoto insisted that he wanted clothes not to be ephemeral, but to last, and even more importantly, he was preoccupied with finding the "essence" of the shirt, the shoulder, the jacket. In describing his ideal garment, he implied that the ephemeral itself could describe something more permanent.[23]

Yamamoto articulated his preference for displaying the inherent characteristics of cloth, be it wrinkles in linen, puckers along a seam, or particular textures, entreating his pattern makers to "listen to" and learn from the material. This is an essentially slow tactic that fashion curator Harold Koda equated with the kimono and regional costume in Japan, where fabric is traditionally wrapped, not cut, becoming a form of "terse expression" that honors the cloth and avoids waste.[24] For cultural reference we can be reminded of how putting on a kimono is a slow process, one that has to be learned and respected. Issey Miyake similarly conducted many experiments with fabric, including innovations from his decades-long collaboration with textile artist Dai Fujiwara. Their "A Piece of Cloth" (APOC) clothing system that could be adapted by wearers, utilized advanced technology, and created innovations including the pleating and simple cutting of synthetic fabrics. The commercially successful Pleats Please line, evoked Mariano Fortuny's early twentieth-century pleated Delphos dresses, but at more accessible prices. Using the long-lasting properties of polyester, a team created garments that were materially and stylistically durable, could fit a variety of body shapes, and were designed for longevity. Similarly, Miyake's 132.5 collection used polyester recycled from plastic bottles to create clothes that were very light, conceived to be like air, seasonless, and intended to be kept for a long time. The technique involved mathematical experiments by Japanese academic Jun Mitani, and complex 3D computer forms, generated from a single piece of flat paper, referencing the slow and careful technique of Japanese origami, paper folding.

Comparatively, scholar Barbara Vinken has observed how Rei Kawakubo "always emphasized that her clothes do not go out of fashion but are made forever."[25] A sense of fashion as existing in the continuous present, and being permanent, rather than ephemeral, is disruptive to the conventional perception of the fashion system. Vinken has related Kawakubo's so-called "negative aesthetic" to the ascetic ideals of Zen Buddhism, which evolved in sixteenth- and seventeenth-century Japan in reaction to the ostentation of Japanese court life. In its renunciation of worldliness, materiality, and status dressing, it can be equated with the *pre*-history of European fashion, reminding us of valuable historical and cultural points of reference for slow rethinking. For Kawakubo, clothes are not intended as a means of influencing others, or even a medium for self-presentation, but rather as a reflection of the thinking of the wearer, and a means of heightening their well-being. Her tactic equates with a slow model, as does the versatility of her clothes, which could be altered by the wearer, even worn inside out, enabling a jacket to become a pullover, and a skirt to turn into a dress. The trait is a "disruptive aesthetics" that effectively designs longevity into garments, whose versatility retain the interest of wearers. It is a characteristic also evident in the work of some younger designers, including those drawing upon their own cultural heritage.

A trench coat created by New York-based American Vietnamese designer Peter Do, from 2022, was designed to be two in one, by the fabric being polished on one side and weathered on the other side (the effect of a resin dye). Do observed that, "Fashion changes all the time … if a garment can allow you to adjust and adapt, then you don't have to constantly seek out newness."[26] Manipulation of textiles into garments using long-established methods of folding, wrapping, twisting, or knotting are also slow techniques, associated with a "zero waste" approach, perpetuated by designers, some who originated in Asia, like New York-based designer Yeohlee Teng. Once described as "one of the most ingenious makers of clothing today,"[27] Yeohlee achieves three-dimensional shapes by a fastidious use of fabric to create clothes that can represent slow principles in their defiance of time and of gender distinction. Referencing long-standing dressing traditions and garments in her native Malaysia, including the sarong, her work emphasizes how looking beyond the fashion and dressing principles familiar in the Global North can inform a slow approach to fashion design. By the end of the twentieth century, a slower disruptive aesthetic was also being demonstrated by some European designers.

Belgian designer Martin Margiela has been credited with initiating "a fashion based on duration, rather than on change."[28] Without being declared as *slow*, Margiela's approach accords with Bruce Goff's sense of the continuous present, mentioned earlier, and provides a significant contrast to the velocity that was building elsewhere in the fashion system. Margiela articulated what has been described as "clothing as habitus" through a practice of repeating favorite designs with slight variations in color or detail over the period of several collections.[29] The focus was on hand making individual garments, an aesthetic of the unfinished or unmade, and styles that did not have to change with fashion seasons. Coined "deconstructivist" fashion by New York fashion photographer Bill Cunningham, and associated specifically with the work of Margiela, Ann Demeulemeester, and Dries Van Noten, it has been described as an auto-critique of the fashion system, or a point when "dress becomes theoretical."[30] Seemingly unfinished garments signified for *The New York Times* fashion critic Amy Spindler, a "coming apart" of fashion's heritage, conceptually and aesthetically, at the end of the twentieth century.[31] It had much greater potential for longevity, as it did not rely on creating a sense of “newness.” While not articulated as a slow approach, Margiela’s “disruptive aesthetics,” and those of his Belgian contemporaries the “Antwerp 6,” can serve as significant points of departure for slower fashion praxis.

Forgotten histories of garments were imaginatively revived by Margiela in unexpected ways. From his first collection in 1988, he disassociated himself with the norms of newness in the fashion system, by revisiting items from his earlier collections. Transformed by hand in the house’s atelier in Paris, his first Artisanal Line “O” reconfigured used clothes acquired at flea markets and elsewhere. For Spring/Summer 1991, ballgowns from the 1950s were cut up, overdyed, and shown worn over blue jeans. This process of transformation, later to be known as upcycling, was not a conscious attempt at sustainability, but reflective of the designer’s interest in the past and in “fashion detritus.”[32] It challenged the historical associations of secondhand clothing with poverty, by giving new life and symbolic value to garments. Margiela’s practices figuratively and economically transformed or “re-fashioned” pre-existing existing garments, and in the process exposed the “traces of slow labor,” that were consciously excluded from fashion production.[33]

Margiela’s design innovation was also demonstrated in a reverence for commonplace items and everyday wear, also foreshadowing how “workwear” brands such as the American Carhartt would gain popularity in the twenty-first century. His famous tabi boots were based on the footwear of Japanese construction workers, farmers, and gardeners. His sweater for Fall/Winter 1991 designed from army socks creatively and economically reconfigured garments from the past. With skill and imagination, the techniques used could be adapted by non-professionals at home, demonstrating how the *practices* of the professional designer could be as instrumental in changing attitudes as in products. Although Margiela only partially reused secondhand garments, his designs nevertheless demonstrate a slow, considered form of construction, and an aesthetic which denied a sense of perfection, and was not tied to any fashion season.

He disturbed the fashion hierarchy further by staging his shows in unexpected and everyday locations. The 1992 collection, for instance, was presented in a Salvation Army sales depot, where the only seating was on furniture amid racks of used clothing. His approach transcended the mere stunt or spectacle. Vinken described Margiela's "rag collecting" not just as a process, but as a philosophy whereby actual items of clothing were re-thought in fashion "as the signs of an individual, unique life and death."[34] These practices were prescient, signaling important directions for slow approaches to fashion.

As Kate Fletcher has noted, slow culture is an invitation to think about systems change in the fashion sector. It is a perspective that must lead, inevitably, to a questioning of the fashion system's underlying values, and its prioritization of profit-driven growth. To achieve ethically inspired change, the area of fashion must first be contextualized alongside other economic, social, and environmental practices. A slow approach to fashion "represents a blatant discontinuity with the practices of today's sector; a break from the values and goals of fast (growth-based) fashion."[35] The approach can often best be facilitated by smaller enterprises, which might then be interconnected, are often run by women, can be located outside of the places and cultures typically associated with the "big F" fashion system, and which honor fabric, and local and domestic means of production. In the process, any sense of one overarching fashion aesthetic is contested, as the following examples from the 1980s and 1990s illustrate.

London-based fashion designer Helen Storey was someone who incorporated existing garments into her collections. Her Second Life project, started in 1990, aimed at taking interesting clothes that had already had a life, and giving them a new one, through what we would now call the process of upcycling. Storey collaborated with Flip, a store in London's Covent Garden selling 1950s American casual clothes. Unusual combinations of materials and textures visually resembling the thrift store styles associated with Grunge in the 1980s were being worn by increasing numbers of young people, as alternatives to mainstream fashion. A collection for Autumn/Winter 1993, for instance, included an outfit that combined a top made of Amish blankets with a skirt of silk chiffon. Second Life employed fashion design graduates, enabling them to be active and creative in ways that would not have been available to them in for-profit companies. As fashion scholar Alison Gill has noted, the "deconstructed" garments that showed up on fashion runways in the early 1990s, with their "images of decay, poverty, and disaffection—appeared to mock fashion from its site of privilege."[36] While acknowledging that such garments were accessible only to those with the cultural capital to know about them and the economic means to purchase them, they prepared the way conceptually and practically for slow praxis to develop for fashion.

A later example, in Florence, Alabama in the United States, that I wrote about in 2008, was developed by designer Natalie Chanin, and provides more perspective on how slow professional praxis for fashion might evolve. For nearly twenty years, as Alabama Chanin, she has contributed to reviving garment making and local cultural heritage in a town previously known for the mass production of T-shirts. Working according to slow principles, her small factory produces around 120 women's garments a day (compared to 120,000 dozen that were manufactured a day by Tee Jays, the company that formerly occupied the space). Garments are cut and machine-made in-house, and hand-sewn items are produced outside by local artisans. The company has a small natural indigo dye house on site, and other colors are dyed in Raleigh, North Carolina. Chanin values the principles of the Slow Food Movement and partners with the Southern Foodways Alliance, which studies, documents, and explores the diverse and changing food cultures of the American South. She also produces sewing kits and holds events to share her commitment to local, home- and community-based garment production. As part of her enterprise, Chanin established Project Threadways, a charity that documents, studies, and interprets the local history, community, and power of fashion and textiles. The breadth of her activities indicates how slow praxis is tactical, with a political agenda of disruption, as distinct from the overarching commercial growth-based strategies of the mainstream fashion system. It is a form of slow politics that was seen increasingly in the twenty-first century.

Slow + Fashion Activism

As the new millennium proceeded, public activism became more evident around the world in reaction to political concerns, and social injustices, as well as anxieties over climate change. In August 2018, fifteen-year-old Greta Thunberg began a protest outside of the Swedish Parliament, holding a sign which read, "School Strike for Climate." As a result, Fridays for Future became an international movement of school students who left their classes that day of the week to participate in demonstrations demanding that political leaders take action to prevent climate change. In 2018, Thunberg addressed the UN Climate Change Conference, and in 2019 she sailed from Sweden to New York by yacht, to avoid carbon-intensive flying, to take to task world leaders at the UN Climate Action Summit. This, effectively slow and non-aggressive, form of everyday activism was characteristic of many other actions, which either used or commented on fashion. In 2021, Thunberg appeared on the cover and was interviewed for the inaugural (August/September) issue of *Vogue Scandinavia*. She had previously been on the covers of British *Vogue* and *Teen Vogue*, amongst other magazines. While some people inevitably criticized Thunberg for associating with the fashion system, her presence signaled her being recognized as "the voice of a generation,"[37] for climate activism, including as it relates to mainstream fashion. While Greta Thunberg is unique in the extent of her individual activism, she has proved to be an important role model, especially for women, and indigenous and young people who continue to have little impact on decision making about the earth's future. When women do make a stand, however, clothing can play a key symbolic role, as it has done historically. We can think, for example of the *bonnet rouge* or "liberty caps" that were knitted by women sitting next to the guillotines during the French Revolution in 1789, or of the white dresses worn with green and purple sashes by Suffragettes in the early twentieth century.

Homemade pink "pussy hats" were worn in January 2017 during the marches in Washington, DC, and elsewhere in the United States, to protest the first election of Donald Trump as president. This example also continues a historical trajectory of the (slow) craft of knitting being used in feminist-initiated craftivism (craft/activism) and demonstrations. The mundane "yellow vest" (*gilet jaune*) came to symbolize economic protests in France, in 2018, just as yellow umbrellas had been part of the movement for political freedom in Hong Kong, suppressed in 2014. The term "fashion activist" was coined and thus given credence in 2010 by Céline Semaan, founder of the New York-based Slow Factory Foundation, in recognition that "fashion creates culture, and culture creates action."[38] Dress and embodiment thus became acknowledged in the twenty-first century as part of political, social, and climate activism, as well as in critiques of the fashion system, focusing especially on the greater well-being of humans and nature, which align with the aims of slow praxis for fashion.

One of the better-known fashion activist organizations, Fashion Revolution, was launched in reaction to the 2013 Rana Plaza disaster. By asking, "Who Made My Clothes?" it has highlighted the lack of transparency surrounding global garment production. Founded in London by Carry Somers and Orsola de Castro, Fashion Revolution describes itself as the world's largest fashion activism movement. Those involved include, amongst others, academics, brands, retailers, fashion producers, policymakers, workers, and wearers, intent on achieving a global fashion industry that conserves and restores the environment and values people over growth and profit. In order to do so, it is committed to bringing about worldwide cultural, industry, and policy change. These objectives are addressed through a decentralized structure of locally based global networks.

Since 2016, it has issued annual *Impact Reports*, which are available for free on its website and provide access and transparency for their activities, their policy advocacy, funding (largely from grants and donations), and impact. In 2017, Fashion Revolution began to issue an annual *Fashion Transparency Index (FTI)* which aimed to make fashion transparent and accountable, enabling knowledge to be freely available about how, where, by whom, and under what conditions clothing is made. In the 2021/2 issue, for example, 250 of the world's largest fashion brands and retailers were ranked according to their level of public disclosure on human rights and the environmental policies, practices, and impacts evident in their own operations and supply chains.

The *FTI* reviewed brands' public disclosure on human rights and environmental issues across 246 indicators in five key areas: Policies & Commitments; Governance; Supply Chain Traceability; Know, Show & Fix, and Spotlight Issues. In 2022 the Spotlight Issues were: Decent work, forced labor, living wages, purchasing practices, unionization and collective bargaining; Gender and racial equality; Sustainable sourcing and materials; Overconsumption and business models; Waste and circularity; Water and chemicals; Climate change and biodiversity. One of the main findings was that progress on transparency in the global fashion industry continued to be too limited. While more brands (48 percent) were disclosing their first-tier suppliers, half still disclosed nothing. Despite mounting evidence of overproduction and clothing waste, most major brands (85 percent) did not publicize their annual production volumes. The overall conditions and payment of workers also remained murky across the industry. Summing up this very detailed and valuable research, Aruna Kashyap, Associate Director (Corporate Accountability), Economic Justice and Rights Division at Human Rights Watch, was quoted in the report as observing that "Transparency needs to be the cornerstone of any serious effort by brands to build a supply chain free from human rights abuses."[39]

At the time of writing, the 2022 FABRIC Act, proposing federal legislation for pay and conditions for garment workers, including more domestic manufacture, is awaiting ratification by the U.S. Congress. One of its champions is Remake, a global advocacy organization involved in fighting for fair pay and climate justice in the clothing industry. PayUp Fashion is a similar global coalition fighting for workers' rights, initiated in 2020 in response to a refusal by many fashion manufacturers to pay for completed clothing orders as the COVID-19 pandemic began and sales dropped. These are examples of targeted slow activism in fashion, which recognize that change needs the investment of time. For, as writer Rebecca Solnit has commented, "every protest shifts the world's balance," or has the potential to do so.[40] Modes of resistance in one place, even when repressed, can leap borders and impact other parts of the world and even other causes.

These observations also contribute to a shared sense of a world in transition. Academic Arturo Escobar, amongst others, has noted how "transition imaginaries" have been formulated for several decades. Reflecting Ivan Illich's (1973) argument for a transition from industrial to convivial societies,[41] they resonate with the aspirations of slow praxis. Transition discourses (TDS) argue that contemporary ecological and social crises are inseparable from dominant models of social life, whether categorized as industrialism, capitalism, modernity, (neo-) liberalism, anthropocentrism, rationalism, patriarchy, secularism, or Judeo-Christian civilization. Most TDS share the contention that we need to step outside existing epistemic boundaries if we truly want to strive for worlds and practices capable of bringing about the significant transformations seen as needed.

For fashion as a practice, change can be activated via modest actions. British scholar Fiona Hackney and her colleagues undertook a wardrobe studies research project, based on my premise of "slow + fashion—women's wisdom," and the value of everyday practices, to uncover "sensibility for sustainable clothing, care and quiet activism."[42] Recognizing the importance of clothes for social, emotional, and psychological identities, they sought "an alternative sensibility of fashion whereby fashion consciousness is reimagined as sustainability consciousness."[43] Fashion can and should be defined and represented as individual choice, not primarily by an overarching and economic profit and growth-based fashion system. A slow praxis for fashion advocates agency, whereby groups of people choose what they wear and how they look, based on their own principles, rather than as determined by the profit-driven global fashion system ("big F" fashion). It resonates with the way that, in the past, counter-cultural, alternative, anti-fashion, and political groups have represented their beliefs through their appearance. A slow approach to fashion emphasizes greater thought about what we wear, how our clothes are made, where, and by whom, how long we keep garments and what we do with them when we no longer want them.

It also demands different perspectives and worldviews from those propagated by the mainstream fashion system. This concept serves as a valuable segue to Section 3, where we consider the redirection required for a slow praxis to evolve for fashion.

3
REDIRECTION

In 2008, I questioned whether applying the concept of slow was an oxymoron or a promise for a more caring future for fashion. Returning to the subject now, over fifteen years later, not only has my response to the question changed, but I recognize that the question needs to be posed differently. It is important to reinforce how the term "fashion" has more than one definition and needs to be examined carefully. The "big F," consumer-driven fashion system, is not the only designation to be made for fashion. From a slow perspective "fashion" can be expressed beyond what people spend their money on, consume, and ultimately throw away. This alternative, "small f" fashion concentrates more on the *practice* of fashion, as a pleasurable act of choosing and dressing, which can demonstrate people's values, their sense of hope and agency. It argues that "fashion" is not only to be defined by the products and mandates of the fashion system. Over the last fifteen years, and while researching and writing this book, it has become increasingly evident to me that a slow approach to fashion is ultimately at odds with the overarching goals of profit and growth of the global ("big F") fashion system.

As Manzini and Jégou have observed, however tomorrow unfolds, it will be built on what is produced *today*, how, by whom, and according to the underlying intentions.[1] But in looking at what might come next, we must also acknowledge the fashion system's ongoing obsession with the future.

Fashion Futures

When the twenty-first century began, one of the shared visions of the future carried a sense of foreboding and dread in its wake. The future had come to feel overwhelming, exacerbated by an excess of media information having intensified a feeling of stress. That sensibility was encapsulated in 2010 by philosopher and cultural critic Slavoj Žižek, whose book *Living in the End Times* (2010), identified four horsemen of a coming apocalypse, characterized by global ecological crisis, economic imbalances, exploding social divisions, and biogenetic revolution. Ten years later, activist social movements such as #MeToo, Black Lives Matter, and Extinction Rebellion were energetically evident around the globe. The fashion system took note. Demna (Gvasalia), then creative director of Balenciaga, staged his Autumn/Winter 2020/1 show against an apocalyptic backdrop of fiery red skies reflected in flooded water through which models trudged with gloomy resolve. Reflecting on this show, Caroline Evans noted that while the pessimism of end times felt particularly relevant in the moment, it was a long-lived idea, found in the eschatology of most world religions.[2] Gloom in the current fashion system was also being tempered by hope, vested in plans for ethical action.

In 2010, the UK-based international organization Forum for the Future launched the report of a joint initiative with Levi Strauss & Co. Using the creative and exploratory process of futures thinking, it considered how climate change, resource shortages, population growth, and other factors would impact the future of the fashion industry, from the production of raw materials, to manufacturing and sales, through to the use and the end of a product's life. Four global scenarios of future worlds were developed as plausible new business models to take products and services towards a more sustainable future from 2025. Each provided overlapping challenges to stimulate new ideas, with climate change and its effects being a top priority. The first was "slow is beautiful," intriguingly proposed as a scenario for a world "of political collaboration and global trade where slow and sustainable is fashionable."

The slow is beautiful scenario embraced a new ethic of "luxury," defined by items that were "good for people and the planet," and by conscientious consumers who would have succeeded in demanding transparency from fashion businesses. Clothes would still be produced globally, but would arrive slowly to market, from production companies that would pay their workers a living wage. Africa would have developed an extensive trade in sustainable cotton, synthetic fabrics would be created cleanly from sustainable resources, and new technology would enable some clothes to monitor people's health. Draconian legislation would have forced individuals to diminish their carbon footprints, by buying clothes that lasted and required less cleaning. Clothes would be washed with cold water without the addition of harmful chemicals. To avoid the high costs of transportation, there would be more local shopping. The latter encompassed vintage clothes, bought in shops or online, as well as handcrafted garments from around the world. The scenario did not directly address how fashions would be created and circulated, other than to speculate that as refugees of climate change began to flee to safer areas, they would take their local fashions with them. While "slow is beautiful" came closest to the principles being explored in this book, an expectation that any part of the scenario could be activated by 2025 was wildly optimistic. Fast planning had become the norm for fashion businesses, an approach contrary to the greater time needed for slow ethical strategies to be developed, implemented, and sustained. The fashion industry also needed longer-term approaches and altogether tougher measures that targeted the harmful impact of fashion production directly on the climate.

Climate Change

According to the 2020 *Fashion on Climate* report, the global fashion industry produced around 2.1 billion tonnes (metric tons) of GHG (greenhouse gas) emissions in 2018, equaling 4% of annual world production, bringing the planet dangerously close to catastrophic warming conditions. Produced by McKinsey & Co in partnership with the Global Fashion Agenda (GFA), the report aimed at guiding and mobilizing global fashion executives to take bold action to ensure greater sustainability practices in their companies. Framing itself in the context of the COVID-19 pandemic and the protests associated with Black Lives Matter, it highlighted the interconnectedness of human lives and the need to address the social concerns that pervaded communities and the fashion industry. Policymakers were documented as refocusing on sustainability in their post-pandemic recovery efforts. But the report also pointed out that the pace of decarbonization efforts needed to accelerate to achieve a reduction of global warming to the 1.5 degrees targeted by the 2015 United Nations Framework Convention on Climate Change (UNFCCC) Paris Climate Change Agreement (enforced by signatories in November 2016) (estimated elsewhere as a need to reduce emissions by 43 percent by 2030). It noted how around only fifty fashion companies had committed to the science-based targets aligned with the agreement. The conclusion was that how value was defined had to be decoupled from volume growth by all parties implicated: brands, and retailers, companies, and consumers. While circular business models were championed in the report, the advocacy organization Remake warned in its *2022 Fashion Accountability Report* of the dangers of circularity washing. No company had truly embraced the reality that degrowth was required. While resale, recycling, and repair services to customers may have increased, degrowth and the reduction of the production of more new clothes did not align with profit-driven interests. More optimistically, the report noted that fashion policy focusing on garment workers' protection had replaced transparency as the dominant mode of change, as citizens turned to their governments when companies failed to pay living wages to workers. But a more fundamental shift in mindset about fashion was also needed, which a slow approach could support.

Renowned eco-philosopher, activist, and scholar, Joanna Macy has written of the need to address the climate crisis as a spiritual path, by which humans recognize their interconnectedness with one another and with nature. While her ideas were founded on her own Buddhist beliefs, they also deserve attention from non-Buddhists. A slower approach to fashion must be holistic and address the connections between fashionable garments, their origins, journeys, and the people and practices involved in their production and wear, including the consequences of wider decision making. As Otto von Busch has noted, any serious discussion around fashion must begin with the question "What is to be sustained?" His own answer is informed by Felix Guattari's taxonomy of three ecological registers: the environment (nature), human relations (social), and human subjectivity (mental), all of which reference social and collective dimensions of injustice. These registers characterize slow praxis for fashion, whereby social relations support sustainable practices, rather than prioritizing the consumption of so-called sustainable products. Here, and for context, we must remind ourselves that the millennium framing concept of the Anthropocene has defined the period since the 1950s as one when human actions have transformed landscapes, ecosystems, and the distribution of species detrimentally. Some scholars have also recast this time as the Capitaloscene, where the priorities of capital, dating back to the Industrial Revolution in Europe, should be recognized as the driving force for subsequent negative environmental and ecological change. It proves a sharp reminder that a slow approach to fashion looks beyond market-driven goals.

Fashion Degrowth

Achieving slow praxis for fashion cannot ignore the fact that the fashion system is driven by economics. As Elizabeth Wilson's much quoted statement declared, "Fashion *speaks* capitalism," but in the process "maims, kills, appropriates, lays waste."[3] Fashion, like ideas of progress, has become tied to economic growth in a societal narrative where consuming more is promoted as being better than the opposite. But in material terms, every unit of growth uses up resources, and creates waste.

A slow approach to fashion cannot endorse economic models dominated by continuous expansion, as Kate Fletcher has emphasized. Fletcher has advocated for slow, not as a business model tied to a specific existing set of economic priorities, but as an alternative to a capital-driven approach. Thus, slow *praxis* for fashion is not predicated on the consumption of more newly made products. Fletcher's perspectives were informed by economist Herman E. Daly, who advocated "post-growth" or "steady state" economics, which could develop qualitatively without growing quantitatively. It should be emphasized that models of a (slower) fashion economy that are predicated on a more integrated picture of social welfare, challenge the classical economic model based on the increase of market value by GDP. While GDP is widely used to measure economic activity, it concentrates on market and production, rather than on the well-being of people, their quality of life, and other factors that are not captured by monetary-based statistics. Scholars and economists have recognized the limitations of GDP strategy, especially following the global financial crisis of 2008, which led to strategies and modes of assessment that give greater attention to human welfare, and provide more opportunities for reflection. As design theorist John Thackara observed, "we've been addressing symptoms, but not their principal cause—an economic system whose core logic is perpetual growth in a finite world."[4] The ideas of Herman Daly, and others who proposed replacing GDP with an Index of Sustainable Economic Welfare (ISEW), which takes various negative values into account as well as positive ones, come closest to a slow approach to fashion economics. Recently, Japanese philosopher Kōhei Saitō used the concept of slowing down powerfully to argue for degrowth, based on the work of Karl Marx and a revised vision of communism, to address the climate crisis of our times.[5]

The slow economic principles developed by Chilean economist Manfred Max-Neef can also inform a slower approach to fashion. He defined "fundamental human needs," non-hierarchically as Being, Having, Doing, and Interacting, characteristics that fashion educator Timo Rissanen highlighted as having the possibility to transform fashion "from a potential pseudo-satisfier to a satisfier."[6] Max-Neef and his co-author physicist Philip B. Smith expressed the belief that, "to achieve an acceptable human community, society must shift its values away from hardness, aggressiveness and competitiveness toward gentleness, compassion and sharing; i.e. away from 'masculine' values toward 'feminine' values."[7] Smith advocated for values such as empathy and sensitivity that are associated with the socially constructed (rather than merely biologically determined) factors related to the feminine (which, it should be noted, can be exhibited by women or by men). In terms of implementation, and building on Max-Neef, British economist Kate Raworth's Doughnut approach to economics sets out a new agenda for the twenty-first century that balanced essential human needs and planetary boundaries. Raworth advocated moving away from the economic policy invented in the 1930s, based on GDP, which had underpinned the development of mass-consumerism in the 1960s. It had produced what French philosopher Giles Lipovetsky, described as a (Western) "society restructured from top to bottom by the attractive and the ephemeral—by the very logic of fashion."[8]

Raworth argues that to thrive and to unleash our potential, humans need to overcome a structural dependency on growth. While growth is a natural stage that leads to maturity, it is only in maturity, not in growth, that anything can thrive for a long time. Raworth advocates for humans to be more agnostic about growth, not always seeking more. She employs a diagram of a ring doughnut, as a visual metaphor for an ideal economy. It is used to indicate how as vast amounts of wealth in the world accrued to the global 1 percent, many other people fall into the shortfall hole of "critical human deprivation" in the center of the doughnut diagram. For a balanced and equitable humanity, the people in the "hole" must be able to progress to "the safe and just space for humanity" of the outer ring.[9] Towards a solution, Raworth proposes ways of thinking that move from twentieth-century to twenty-first-century economics, which for us can also undergird a slow approach to fashion. She expresses the need to change goals of growth to the achievement of dynamic balance, which takes a big picture and longer-term approach to thinking and planning. Human nature must be nurtured to become more socially adaptable, more knowledgeable about systems, and appreciative of dynamic complexity. Economies must be designed more for distribution, and creation aimed at regeneration, employing a cyclical rather than a linear approach, to meet the needs of people in the twenty-first century. Raworth cites facilities such as blockchain, the digital peer-to-peer decentralized platform that can track all types of value exchange between people, towards greater transparency and reduced intermediation. Another example of decentralization is "care-currency," where care is earned by giving care to others. While cautioning that such schemes must serve to reinforce, not institutionalize, the fundamental human instinct to care for others, it offers an alternative that is not predicated on capital growth. In the fashion system, care can be startlingly absent. What would be required are slower, more attentive, and more caring attitudes not just towards what is worn, but also an expanded recognition of how "fashion" is defined and produced, and by whom. In other words, shifts in mindset, which would impact practices, to establish fashion praxis informed by slow principles. It is all too evident that the solution cannot be found with governments or within the fashion system alone, if at all.

Caring

In 2018, the choice by Melania Trump, as first lady of the United States, to wear a US$39 parka jacket from Zara, emblazoned on the back with "I really don't care, do you?" to visit migrant children at a Texas border detention center, remains a "fashion moment" of the worst sort. It is mentioned here as the antithesis of slow principles and values. The garment, and the wearer, represented how the fashion system, fueled by capitalism, lacked care on many levels, not least about workers, as well as pollution, and waste. As *The Care Manifesto* (The Care Collective, 2020), authored by London-based feminist activists argued, neoliberal capitalism does not and cannot "value personal engagement, emotional connection, commitment, empathy or attentiveness, unless contracted for financial rewards."[10] Kate Raworth is amongst the alternative, socialist, and feminist economists cited in the manifesto, who support economic models where universal care is considered part of the ecology of the living world. Prioritizing care logics over market logics represents a different, more considered, and *slower* perspective on many aspects of life, which give value to the local, and the human. But the belief is also expressed in the manifesto that care and capitalist market logics cannot be reconciled. Care is best delivered with human engagement and emotional attachment, while markets allocate responsibilities based on purchasing power, which overwhelm non-market values. The conclusion was that caring values can only flourish when market metrics and corporate power were eliminated. It was a statement that was highlighted unexpectedly in 2020 when the fashion system, its organizations, and players felt compelled to demonstrate more caring perspectives, in response to Black Lives Matter, and the COVID-19 pandemic.

In the wake of the Black Lives Matter Movement and following the killing of George Floyd by police in Minneapolis in May 2020, the mainstream fashion media in the United States addressed its own lack of diversity in racial representation. On the cover of the July/August 2020 issue of *Vanity Fair*, Black actress Viola Davis was photographed by Black photographer Dario Calmese, her back exposed in a pose reflective of an iconic 1836 photograph of the scarred back of a formerly enslaved man. A subsequent issue featured a posthumous painting, by artist Amy Sherald, of Breonna Taylor, a Black woman recently killed in her home by police. The media-based narrative of fashion in America appeared to be being re-imagined as a more caring and considered form of historical retribution. American *Vogue* had previously employed Tyler Mitchell as the first Black photographer to capture Black celebrity Beyoncé for the cover of its September 2018 issue. But two years later, editor in chief, and by then Condé Nast's worldwide chief content officer, Anna Wintour was criticized in the press for these acknowledgments coming too late. The potential for the fashion system, and its mouthpiece the fashion media, to genuinely care about humanity appeared to be at odds with its overarching profit-driven agenda. By contrast, more meaningful, slower manifestations of fashion's symbolic and emotional significance were being demonstrated by ordinary people coming together. One powerful example was the "million hoodie march" held in New York in 2012 in honor of Trayvon Martin, a Black teenager who was wearing the ubiquitous garment when he was murdered by a white man in a Florida neighborhood.[11]

A slow approach addresses the lack of care in the fashion system, either from outside the system, or from within it. The resolution of the system's problems cannot be addressed effectively by media, business, or government actors, if the actions involved are selective and partial. A defetishization of fashion is required in parallel with increased accountability along the commodity chain, to the benefit of garment workers, including the expansion of laws and regulations that help to deprioritize the neoliberal commercial agenda. The fashion system does not have to lack care, as was demonstrated repeatedly during the COVID-19 pandemic. Early in the lockdown, New York-based fashion designer Kerby Jean-Raymond was reported as having set $50,000 aside for minority and women-owned small creative businesses then in distress. Converting the studio of his Pyer Moss brand into a donation center for N95 masks and latex gloves was for him an "imperfect solution." But the CFDA (Council of Fashion Designers of America) commended his actions as "admirable and inspiring exactly what is needed as we battle the COVID-19 outbreak—especially as numbers of those testing positive are rising at a staggering rate."[12] At the same time, the CFDA and American *Vogue* jointly reinvigorated their The Common Thread initiative, established to support fashion businesses impacted by the 9/11 World Trade Center attack, as a COVID-19 fashion relief fund, in collaboration with Harlem's Fashion Row. New York-based Fashion Girls for Humanity responded at the local level by addressing the severe shortage of PPE (Personal Protective Equipment) in the United States. In less than three months, the women-led initiative became global with more than 100,000 people from 155 countries in Europe, Australia, Asia, South America, Africa, and across the United States having downloaded online mask and gown patterns and viewed how-to-make tutorials. The group also supported small local businesses during the pandemic, by raising funds to have medical gowns produced by women in New York's Garment district.[13] (Many similar actions were also undertaken in other parts of the world.)

Caring provides an important direction for the development of slower praxis for fashion, which must also look beyond the fashion system. Taking care is an ongoing and relational act. It is a cycle of involvement, attention, and responsibility. It encompasses caring *for*, caring *about*, and caring *with*. Caring *for* highlights care for clothes, through processes of cleaning, mending, and other means that can provide greater longevity to material garments. Clothing durability involves work and commitment, much of which takes place in the home, traditionally the key domain of such activities and knowledge. Caring *about* recognizes the origins of clothes, beginning with the natural fabrics and fibers, which come from the earth, and also the workers who produce what we wear. Ayesha Barenblat, founder and CEO of Remake, a global advocacy organization for fair pay and climate justice in the clothing industry, remarked before the pandemic on a 60 percent increase in clothing production worldwide over the previous twenty years. But garments were being kept for half as long, especially in the United States and China, the largest apparel retail markets in the world. To address this hypergrowth, Barenblat advocated for mindful consumerism, a more caring, and distinctly slower, approach of "buying less, buying quality, and making purchases from companies that treat workers fairly and pay living wages."[14] Finally, caring *with* reminds us how clothes can contribute to self-care for human beings, as they did in the pandemic. Clothing can protect the wearer from external conditions, as well as provide comfort and security in times of anxiety or when the body has been harmed or is ill or injured.[15] Fashion *in action* ultimately implicates the clothes we wear.

A caring and slow approach to fashion must begin with the self, with individual commitment and responsibility, which can then be extended collectively to our clothes and their human and natural origins and relationships.

In Westernized societies self-care can be confused with egoism and self-indulgence, but if we look further, to Buddhist beliefs for example, self-care is seen as a fundamental step towards caring for others. During the pandemic, care and self-care became much more essential. As was pointed out, in the helping professions, self-care is "an essential component of prevention of distress, burnout, and impairment." It should not be considered as something "extra" or "nice to do if you have time."[16] A slow approach means returning to fundamentals. Models for more caring and slower praxis for fashion exist outside of the fashion system, and beyond the Global North. The Sanskrit term *Ahimsa*, meaning non-harming of the self and others, which was adopted famously by Mahatma Gandhi, has been applied to the agenda of achieving waste-free fashion design by scholar and designer Şölen Kipöz.[17] The greater mediatization of the fashion system since the late twentieth century, particularly with fast fashion, has contributed to diminishing longer-term relationships between people and what they wear. It is a condition that slowness in fashion can strive to rectify. Its tactic will be to look beyond fashion's primary appeal to the visual sense, to focus on clothes as material garments, rather than simply on images, especially digital images delivered via social media, which have been said to have "flattened fashion."[18]

Sensing

Slowness can be practiced through touch. Emphasizing senses other than the visual challenges notions of the "fashionable" being based largely on image and appearance. It serves to de-emphasize the transitory fashion "look," which also discourages wearers from forming lasting relationships with clothing items. Such prioritization of transitory fashionable appearances relates to the greater reliance on the sense of sight in the modern world. It has been noted that "knowledge ... gleaned by smell or touch or sound, does not always, or even habitually, penetrate the modern consciousness." The same source continues that not only is such knowledge overlooked, but it is also ignored because it "undermines our cherished individualism."[19] In modern culture the senses have been ranked hierarchically according to their immediacy. Sight and hearing were given highest ranking, as they depend on relationships with external objects, operate across distance, and yet can remember at will. Smell was ranked next, which like sound is public and external. Taste and touch were traditionally placed lowest, as both depend on direct physical contact with the world, but are also internalized and private to the subject. Malcolm McCullough has proposed that touch is partly undervalued because the main instruments of touch—the hands—are also underrated. While hands bring us knowledge of the world—they are associated with manual work.[20] In modernity (and in the mass production of fashion items), manual work has been devalued for its productive capacity when compared to machines, which will always produce greater quantity and more "perfect" looking products. Yet valuing touch is essential to slowing down how we choose our clothes and how we wear them.

Instilling slow principles will impact not only fashion's relationship to newness, but encourage stronger physical relationships between people and their clothing items, and build on what already exists. Such relationships were documented, for example, by Sophie Woodward, in her ethnographic investigations of practices of wearing and keeping clothes. Memory is a key factor to what people choose to retain in their wardrobes, as Heike Jenss has explored in her research on vintage style and youth culture.[21] Both sets of scholarly research served to reinforce the significant emotional relationships that people form with what they wear. Alex Nora Esculapio has highlighted the possibilities for emotional durability in fashion, through the work of designers, based on the conceptual framework established by design theorist Jonathan Chapman. Emotional durability overlaps with the aims of slower fashion practices, towards extending the lifetime of garments, and acknowledging and re-thinking the agency of users in fashion activities.[22] For Chapman, "Emotionally durable fashion is adaptable and capable of modification, it uses materials that age well and grow old gracefully, it is designed to be repaired with low levels of skill, and it avoids fleeting trends to occupy a slower and more enriching style space."[23] Chapman handed the responsibility to designers for "making stuff that lasts," in order to reduce the need to consume more. This of course means establishing emotional durability, not just material longevity. A slower approach to fashion advocates for a refocusing of fashion agency onto the wearer and aligns with Kate Fletcher and Anna Fitzpatrick's ideas and actions around longer-lasting clothes. Durability in clothing, they state, relies on a commitment to care, and a delegation of expert knowledge of durability from "professionals and industry to homes and often to women."[24] Their premise was informed by interview-based fieldwork which investigated clothing ideas and practices in the Global South in 2021, specifically in Africa, Latin America, India, and the Aotearoa Maori community, which offered insights to the Global North. Of note is their distinctly slow conclusion that the durability of clothing "is associated with the capacity to act independently of a fashion system and its consumerist priorities."[25]

Writing in 2013, Anna König documented an apparent revival in domestic mending in the UK, mainland Europe, and North America, coinciding with a growing interest in more sustainable material goods.[26] Evidence of the application of techniques such as "visible mending" is attested, for example, through the activities of makers like Kate Sekules, a mender who, at the time of writing, has almost 30,000 social media followers, and has authored a popular book, which details mending history and practice.[27] Like hand knitting, which I mentioned in my 2008 "Slow + Fashion" article, mending is a literally slow technique. Actions of making and recreating can enable a refocusing of how fashion is defined, to include "one-off" garments that are unique but everyday, and often made or adapted by wearers. While such garments are distinct in their making process from custom-made or haute couture items, they are equally particular and individual. Valuing choice, rather than following a commercial mandate to buy new mass-produced clothes, highlights the practical and emotional role of fashion and its collaborative and cooperative nature, especially for and by women.

Women's Wisdom

In seeking a slow praxis for fashion, it is important to look beyond, as well as within, the mainstream fashion system to encompass the actions and ideas of professionals, thinkers, and wearers of clothes around the world. Here I want to highlight, as I did in my 2019 article, how the varied contributions of women to this process have often become obscured, especially in the fashion system's larger corporate contexts. "Women's wisdom," therefore, does not highlight only the literal words and thoughts of women, or intend to imply biological determinism, but highlights a slower, more thoughtful, and collaborative fashion praxis. The term also acknowledges the wisdom of indigenous women around the globe, which is deeply rooted in the earth, and has been passed down between generations. What follows are some contemporary, fashion-related initiatives, offered as examples.

Eileen Fisher, of the eponymous American womenswear brand committed to the environment through sustainability and recycling, and to human rights and the well-being of women and girls, has taken the company's ethos beyond the production of clothes. Her Women Together initiative, launched in March 2019, has provided insights and support for women. Workshops, talks, the first by feminist icon Gloria Steinem, and livestreams aimed at empowering women to find their voices, are held, fueled by Fisher's belief that when women connect with each other a collective energy emerges. The initiative began during the pandemic, when free sessions were hosted twice weekly, enabling women to listen to speakers and to interact with one another. They attracted hundreds of participants from across the United States, from the UK, and from other English-speaking countries. Those attending expressed their gratitude at being able to connect with one another when everyone was stuck inside. This was, and continues to be, slow praxis, aimed at education, well-being, and fostering sustainable economies by women professionals active *within* the fashion system, but not aimed at producing (more) clothes.

In the academy, the wider fashion discourse has been changing, effectively slowing, and becoming more intentional. Conversations, largely instigated by women, and by people outside of the Global North, have challenged previous definitions of *fashion* with the aim of transforming fashion thinking and knowledge-sharing, and who might participate. In February 2021, the Research Collective for Decoloniality and Fashion (RCDF), online Conversations on Decoloniality & Fashion, was established to connect fashion academics and practitioners across time zones, language barriers, and experiences. It aimed (and continues) to establish decolonial and decentralized methods of knowledge-creation and sharing about fashion—through the relational and conversational, the communal and coalitional, and by radical acts of listening across multiple differences. Existing outside of an institution, on a donation basis, it represents a radical shift away from the dominant Eurocentric underpinnings of the fashion system and the fashion academy, by encouraging critical analysis and dialogue from more participants and towards greater diversity. The RCDF engages globally with different temporalities, voices, and ideas, effectively practicing slowness, in its ethical approach to fashion in the everyday. One of its founders, Angela Jansen, has distinguished "fashion" as a noun and a verb,[28] which are important distinctions for slow praxis for fashion.

Fashion as a noun signals the contemporary global fashion system (or "big F" fashion) with its own self-generated temporality, materialized through current styles and "looks," underpinned by an exploitative and destructive capitalist industry. Fashion as a verb ("small f" fashion) is slow, reflecting the different acts of fashioning the body, across the world, respectful of varying times and places. Modernity and capitalism have reinforced the superiority and universality of the global fashion system, and in the process have diminished the recognition of self-fashioning as a practice evident in local cultural contexts across the world. Self-fashioning[29] is an inherent and pleasurable practice of human beings, which can be praxis, building on slower attitudes to what we wear. Slow thinking about fashion demands different perspectives, respects different worldviews and uses more fitting terminology. Fashion scholar Djurdja Bartlett noted the preference, for example, by some early twenty-first-century philosophers, for the concept of "mondialization," over globalization, considering the latter too narrow and dismissive "of culture and history in favor of economics and geography."[30] In this process, the Earth has become a point of reference for women, and a connection with indigenous knowledge, and slow thinking. In the age of the Anthropocene, as human activity is increasingly recognized as having an adverse impact on the planet's climate and ecosystems, recognizing and addressing the Earth becomes increasingly important and urgent.

Earth

In the 1960s, British chemist James Lovelock posited his, then controversial, Gaia hypothesis that the Earth and its biological systems functioned as a huge single entity. More recently, the concept has regained attention in the context of the climate crisis. Named after the Greek goddess of the Earth, Gaia reinforced the ancient connections between women and the planet, and the need to care for nature and the environment. Organizations, such as the Women's Earth Alliance, founded in 2006, demonstrated through their mission and activities, the undertakings of women working at the grassroots with natural resources. The Earth has also been recognized and highlighted creatively as part of slower approaches to fashion. For example, it provided the focus for the exhibition *Earth Matters*, co-curated by Lidewij Edelkoort and Philip Fimmano in 2017, which showcased diverse examples of work from designers and artists worldwide.[31] Included was upcycling by Eileen Fisher, emphasizing the brand's Vision 2020 commitment to sustainability. Dosa, by Los Angeles-based Christina Kim, featured craft communities from India to Mexico, via Cambodia, Columbia, and Turkey, working with scraps of fabric and remnants of yarn, reflecting slower making strategies. Dutch designer Birgitta de Vos referenced the need for taking time and going slow, positioning making clothes as an act of contemplation. A similar perspective underpinned Golden Journey, a non-commercial apparel initiative from the Dutch clothing collective Painted Series. Their technique, described as "meditative mending," corresponds to domestic practices, and more specifically to the traditional Japanese *kintsugi* (golden joinery) technique, used to repair broken pottery with strips of lacquer, dusted with gold, silver, or platinum. These are valuable examples of slow techniques that can be practiced effectively by anyone, as they have been for centuries.

Physical earth has also literally been incorporated into the work of contemporary fashion designers. Most famously, British-based Hussein Chalayan buried his graduate collection, "The Tangent Flows," in 1993. For Chinese designer Ma Ke, earth was used in her *Wuyong/the Earth* collection to smear garments to form a connection with traditional Chinese crafts, history, and a search for more informed and ethically conscious fashion practices. Calling it "dirty fashion," critic Calvin Hui described the clothes as being underpinned symbolically by "a sense of history and memory, turning it from a garment that forgets to a garment that remembers."[32] Hui accused Ma Ke of aestheticizing and romanticizing dirt, but also described her work as being emblematic of "slowness, duration, permanence and history."[33] Subsequently, the designer's interest in quotidian dress practices was reflected in *My Land, My People* (begun in 2011), a collection of photographs, garments, and wearer ethnographies, whose subjects lived in the remote mountain areas of Gansu province in northeast China, and Sichuan in the southwest. Many of the clothing items were dirty and ragged, having been repaired frequently and passed between generations, but served as reminders of the everyday value of the clothes. They were the only garments that the wearers owned, providing an interface of sorts between their human bodies and the Earth on which they lived and worked. The dilution and erasure of connections between human lives and the earth is an outcome of faster urban lifestyles. It recalls, for example, Kate Fletcher's beautiful account of clothes being muddied when worn in the English countryside, reminding us how garments can reconnect us with the Earth, the original source of our fabrics and garments.[34]

Kate Fletcher and Mathilda Tham took *Earth Logic* as the title and focus for their 2019 *Fashion Action Research Plan*. In it they advocate staying with "the trouble," honoring Donna Haraway's commitment to the uncompromising task of living better together on a damaged planet.[35] To this end, they argue that the economic growth logic that drives the fashion sector needs to be profoundly rethought, through systemic work. (Their collaborative work is also accessible through the Union of Concerned Researchers in Fashion, a global network comprising over 400 researchers and practitioners in fashion and sustainability, founded in 2018.) The *Earth Logic* plan comprises eight explicit values: multiple centers; interdependency; diverse ways of knowing; co-creation; action research; grounded imagination; care of world; care of self.[36] The values informed six holistic landscapes for fashion action research. The first three: less, local, and plural, focus directly on fashion actions. Less is characterized as the largest provocation associated with the transition to sustainability, but also the one most likely to imply techno-fixes. The authors acknowledge the possible social-economic consequences of less production, especially for employees in the textile and clothing industries. But they also point to how people are experiencing unease with living with too much, citing the popular and global success of Japanese cleaning consultant Marie Kondo's approach to tidying. Reflecting on the local, they highlight not only the economic and political power inside communities, but the importance to people of a sense of identity rooted in culture and belief systems. Fletcher and Tham's fourth landscape for fashion action research—learning, also deserves our attention (the fifth and sixth being language and governance). Their underlying sense of the plural resonates with the ideas of other thinkers, such as Arturo Escobar's notion of the pluriverse.

Education

Like Arturo Escobar, and many of the writers whose work has informed this book directly and indirectly, Fletcher and Tham are both educators as well as scholars and writers, involved in institutional-based education in colleges and universities, and internationally within wider community activities. Fletcher's Local Wisdom project, documented in her book, *Craft of Use: Post-Growth Fashion* (2016), demonstrated how research and discovery informs and educates both in institutions of learning and more broadly. There are now an increasing number of professionals and teachers whose work can contribute to a *slow* praxis for fashion, for new and potentially sustainable economies and ideas of well-being. They offer informed, creative, critical, and *thoughtful* approaches to how fashion might be identified and defined going forward. UK educator Amy Twigger Holroyd and her collaborators began Fashion Fictions, an international participatory project, in 2020. Inventively, it brought together people from different backgrounds and places "to generate, experience, and reflect on engaging fictional visions of sustainable fashion cultures and systems."[37] Methodologically, it demonstrates the power and possibility of exploration and imagination, and the broader aim of achieving the degrowth needed to counter the effects of climate change. Nowadays, such projects and ideas can be shared so readily via electronic media.

Designer Ma Ke's fashion practices and ideas, for example, have been distributed virtually and through in person lectures and prestigious international events. In October 2009, she presented a manifesto, Design with Conscience, Live with Simplicity to the Icograda World Design Congress, in Beijing. Part autobiography and part polemic, informed by Chinese and Western thinking, it shared what she felt might be learned from rapidly vanishing aspects of ordinary and everyday life in rural China. Ma Ke described her own infatuation with handmade things since childhood and her adoption of a "slow life."[38] It is an example of how the manifesto has become popular in the fashion system, issued by brands and individuals, and in fashion education. Lidewij Edelkoort's "Anti_Fashion: Ten Reasons Why the Fashion System Is Obsolete" (2015) challenged what she observed as an internationally reiterative yet obsolescent model of fashion design education aimed at creating individualistic and narcissistic star designers. Fashion creation is, after all, a collective endeavor. Edelkoort praised some designers, including women, who did not make fashion-induced change for changes sake in their work, thus effectively declaring "newness a thing of the past." She foresaw a "new consumer" who will have an interest in clothes, rather than *fashion*, which may be shared, rented, loaned, found, handed down, or transformed. While Edelkoort has been criticized for conforming to the system that she was critiquing (as well as selling copies of her four-page manifesto for 50 euros each), her words were thought-provoking. Although, as Marco Pecorari later noted, the term manifesto was becoming an allusion to a vision rather than a practice, more synonymous with performance rather than action.[39] Summing up Edlekoort's manifesto, fashion scholar Christopher Breward reflected that its demands for deeper engagement with fashion offered some common ground in the search "for quality and insight, for a version of 'slow fashion'."[40]

Fashion educator Timo Rissanen produced a manifesto in 2017 that emphasized the need for fashion schools to cultivate an ethos of collectivity, rather than individuality, while focusing on equity, inclusion, and decolonization. Rissanen defined "everyone a user of fashion," but pointed out that aspects of "fashion usership," including how clothes are chosen, laundered, and disposed of, verge on the automatic, and would benefit from more thought in daily life.[41] He noted that both fashion and sustainability concerned themselves with the future, but the one (fashion) focused on two years hence, and the other (sustainability) needed much longer spans of time.[42] Rissanen advocated for fashion design being informed by a more complex sense of time that was circular and layered, instead of the modern linear model. (Rissanen's re-imagining of fashion design's primary function to be a satisfier of fundamental human needs, may also be compared to the Slow Food movement's emphasis on the *pleasure* of food.[43]) The motivation of *having* for its own sake leads to overconsumption. By contrast, there is satisfaction to be gained from collaboration and sharing. Rissanen encourages a new critical and collective fashion system that embodies courageous imagination, and new forms of wisdom.

Manifestos have also called for degrowth. Philosopher Kōhei Saitō's book *Slow Down* (2024) mentioned earlier, is subtitled *The Degrowth Manifesto.* Anthropologist Sandra Niessen adopted the neologism "defashion," coined in 2022 by the activist group Fashion Act Now as a goal for 2030, for her "Defining defashion: A manifesto for degrowth."[44] This manifesto provides an apt conclusion to slow praxis as redirection for fashion. Niessen calls for an urgent paradigmatic shift, whereby the fashion industry prioritizes the well-being of people, their lifeways, and the Earth. Like degrowth, defashioning prioritizes a deep reduction in material and energy in clothing production, and a transition to post-fashion clothing systems that are regenerative, local, fair, nurturing, and provide only what is sufficient for the needs of communities. The principles of Fashion Act Now equate with the slow approach advocated in this book. It calls for a clothing commons that replaces the current monolithic fashion system with a pluriverse of clothing systems that are fair, local, decolonial, and profoundly respectful and nurturing. Defashion references failures by national governments and intergovernmental bodies to address losses of culture and biodiversity, in which the fashion industry is deeply implicated. It is a radical approach that will require revolutionary changes to the global economic system. Niessen acknowledges that the term *fashion* is difficult to negotiate. While it has universal application, its surrounding culture is typically focused on "big F" fashion, on the Western-based global fashion system, controlled in the Global North, which operates within a capitalist imperative of economic growth. The resulting call is for the dismantling of a system that no longer meets the needs of people, cultures, and the planet. It recognizes that ("small f") fashion can, and should, be prioritized to include the existence of a variety of systems and universal practices, that coexist around the world, for dressing the body.

So, to reiterate, to view fashion through a slow lens, highlighting personal creativity and style, not commerce and trade, changes our perspective, and emphasizes the actions and agency of wearers. It prioritizes the well-being of humans, nature, and our wider environment. Being able to choose what to wear is pleasurable, freeing, and creative, and should not be the provenance of a global, commercial, and profit-driven industry. In this book, an investigation of slow for fashion has been offered as an ethical and creative praxis and response to the sense of disquiet and anxiety that underlies choices about what to wear, and about how, where, and how much clothing is produced in the name of fashion. It is a responsibility which we all share, and which can and must result in action.

A CALL TO ACTION

This final section is in the form of a list of slow actions for fashion, developed from the preceding pages of the book, which are intended as reflections and provocations for readers, especially those located in the Global North (listed in alphabetical order).

Advocacy

We can all advocate for slow approaches to fashion, which will vary in form depending on where and who we are.

Attention

Slow praxis for fashion needs attention and focus in order to be developed, and for its conception and application to be effective.

Caring

Greater care can and must be applied throughout the fashion system, by individuals, groups, institutions, governments and more, and must pertain to humans, nature, and the environment, as well as clothes.

Collective

Slow approaches to fashion creation are collective and collaborative, acknowledging and valuing the role of individual producers and wearers, but also the fact that we are all interdependent.

Consumer Citizens

As citizens, consumers must advocate for slow approaches to fashion, through their purchasing practices, and by lobbying large corporations and government bodies towards greater transparency and more sustainable and honest practices.

Consumption

If you choose to buy clothes, follow the advice of Ayesha Barenblat of Remake to buy less, buy quality, and purchase from companies that treat workers fairly and pay living wages.

Disruptive Aesthetics

Disruptive aesthetics are slow, and create more versatile and original garments that do not conform to the dictates of mainstream fashion and encourage more creative ways of dressing.

Durability

Recognizing the physical and emotional durability of clothing is central to slow praxis for fashion, and counter to the transitory aims of fast fashion.

Earth

The Earth is an important point of reference in reframing fashion perspectives.

Education

Nuanced, informed, and up-to-date education is essential.

Imagination

Offers potential for revised and expansive thought and action. Fashion must be reimagined as informed praxis, not just as the purchase of more prescribed commodities.

Influencers

Influencers are needed, who are informed and committed to spreading an understanding of how to develop and achieve slow praxis for fashion.

Investment

Whatever their price, modest or more substantial, we must treat our clothing purchases as investments, not as perishables.

Less

Less—not more—must be the focus for producers and wearers.

Local

Value the local, including the economic and political power inside communities, and the importance to people of a sense of identity rooted in culture and belief systems, all of which impact clothes.

Longevity

Many clothes need to be made to last longer and wearers should use their clothes for longer periods of time than they do.

Pleasure

Making sound fashion choices can foreground a greater sense of pleasure in what we wear.

Plural

This is a combined effort.

Quality

As Kate Fletcher noted, slow designing, producing, consuming, and living better are not time based, but quality based.

Redefinition

The fashion system and "big F" fashion does not have to dominate how fashion is defined, wearers must take agency in their fashion and clothing decisions.

Reduce

This is essential—the world already has enough clothes for everyone.

Repair

Repair can be creative as well as practical, resulting in unique garments.

Style

Developing personal style is slow; it is not defined by time, but by what wearers choose, to suit their preferences, wishes, and personalities.

Systems Change

The fashion system must change to prioritize its responsibilities to people and the planet, over and above achieving increased economic profit for the few.

Time

A slow approach to fashion will disrupt existing "big F" fashion time, to move from being fast and market driven, to being much longer term.

Touch

A slow approach considers all sensory relations to what we wear, not just what we see and how we look.

Use-less

Most people can use fewer clothes—there are too many clothes that remain unworn in the homes, wardrobes, closets, and drawers of individuals.

Value

Slow praxis for fashion advocates quality, not quantity, and valuing clothes by how much they mean to wearers, not by their price tag.

Well-being

A slow approach to fashion considers the well-being of garment workers, wearers, and of the Earth.

Women's wisdom

The work and ideas of women as professionals, practitioners, and wearers of clothes can offer directions, which are largely absent from or obscured in much of the corporate "big F" fashion system.

NOTES

Preface

1 "Slow Listening," *Bureau for Listening.* Available online.

2 Beth Crane, "Welcome to Slow Living Ldn," *slow living ldn*, 2018. Available online.

Introduction

1 Ezio Manzini and François Jégou, *Sustainable Everyday: Scenarios of Urban Life* (Milan: Edizioni Ambiente, 2003), produced by La Triennale di Milano as part of the XX International Exposition on "Memory and the Future."

2 Carl Honoré, *In Praise of Slowness: How a Worldwide Movement is Challenging the Cult of Speed* (London: Orion Books, 2005), 13 [First published in French in 1995].

3 Hazel Clark, "Eco Fashion—Conviction or Conceit?," an unpublished paper presented at the *Twentieth Annual Conference Association of Art Historians*, Birmingham Polytechnic, UK, April 1994.

4 Wendy Parkins and Geoffrey Craig, *Slow Living* (Oxford and New York: Berg, 2006), ix.

5 Hazel Clark, "Slow + Fashion: An Oxymoron—or a Promise for the Future ...?" *Fashion Theory: The Journal of Dress, Body and Culture* 12, no. 4 (2008): 429.

6 Rebecca Earley, "Well-Fashioned: Eco Style in the UK Crafts Council, London 2006 Interview with Rebecca Earley—Curator," 2006. Available online.

7 Kate Fletcher, *Sustainable Fashion and Textiles: Design Journeys* (London and Sterling, VA: Earthscan, 2008), 175.

8 Kate Fletcher, "Slow Fashion," *The Ecologist*, June 1, 2007. Available online.

9 Kate Fletcher, "Slow Fashion: An Invitation for Systems Change," *Fashion Practice: The Journal of Design, Creative Process & The Fashion Industry* 2, no. 2 (2010): 264.

10 Fletcher, "Slow Fashion: An Invitation for Systems Change," 262.

11 Alastair Fuad-Luke, "Rethinking Slowtopia," in Şölen Kipoz (ed.) *Slowness in Fashion* (Sofia: Dixi Books, 2020), 25 and 27.

12 Alastair Fuad-Luke, "'Slow Design': A Paradigm Shift in Design Philosophy?" Development by Design, dyd02 Conference, Bangalore, India, 2002.

13 Cheryl Buckley and Hazel Clark, *Fashion in Everyday Life: London and New York* (Bloomsbury: London and New York, 2017), 1.

14 Sophie Woodward, *Why Women Wear What They Wear* (Oxford and New York: Berg, 2007); Sophie Woodward and Daniel Miller, *Blue Jeans: The Art of the Ordinary* (Berkeley, CA: University of California Press, 2012).

15 Hazel Clark, "Slow + Fashion—Women's Wisdom," *Fashion Practice: The Journal of Design, Creative Process and the Fashion Industry* 11, no. 3 (2019): 309–27.

16 Michel de Certeau, "The Practice of Everyday Life: 'Making Do': Uses and Tactics," in Gabrielle M. Spiegel (ed.) *Practicing History: New Directions in Historical Writing after the Linguistic Turn* (London and New York: Routledge, 2005), 213–23.

17 Marcus Fairs, "Li Edelkoort Proposes 'World Hope Forum' in a Manifesto for Rebuilding Society after Coronavirus." *vdf: virtual design festival*, April 15, 2020. Available online.

Chapter 1

1 Elliot Hoste, "Temu's $0 Fur Boots Are the Bottom of the Fast Fashion Barrel," *Dazed*, March 12, 2024. Available online.

2 Alain Badiou, *Infinite Thought* (Continuum: London and New York, 2005), 38.

3 Anja Aronowsky Cronberg, "Can Fashion Ever Be Democratic," *Vestoj*, January 13, 2010.

4 Anne-Marie Schiro, "Fashion; Two New Stores that Cruise Fashion's Fast Lane," *The New York Times*, December 31, 1989. Available online.

5 Miles Socha, "Seminal Moment: When Karl Lagerfeld Embraced H&M," *WWD*, May 13, 2020. Available online.

6 Ruth La Ferla, "'Cheap Chic' Draws Crowds on 5th Ave," *The New York Times*, April 11, 2000. Available online.

7 Kate Fletcher, "Fashion, Fast and Slow," in Caroline Evans and Alessandra Vaccari (eds) *Time in Fashion: Industrial, Antilinear and Uchronic Temporalities* (London: Bloomsbury, 2020), 71.

8 Andrew Brooks, *Clothing Poverty: The Hidden World of Fast Fashion and Second-Hand Clothes* (London: Zed Books, 2019), 58.

9 Sarah Jackson, "China: Shein Factory Employees Work 18 Hours a Day with No Weekends Earning Just Two Cents per Item, Report Finds," *Business & Human Rights Resource Centre*, October 16, 2022. Available online.

10 Sanchita Saxena and Salil Tripathi, *Rana Plaza 10 Years On—Lessons for Human Rights and Business* (London: IHRB, 2023).

11 Teri Agins, *The End of Fashion: How Marketing Changed the Clothing Business Forever* (New York: William Morrow & Co., 1999), 13.

12 Guy Debord, *The Society of the Spectacle*, trans. Ken Knabb (Berkeley, CA: Bureau of Public Secrets, [1967], 2014), 11.

13 "Fast Fashion's Addiction to Synthetic Fibres," *Ethical Consumer,* April 6, 2021. Available online.

14 For more see David Brunnschweiler and John Hearle (eds), *Polyester: Tomorrow's Ideas and Profits: Fifty Years of Achievement* (Manchester: The Textile Institute, 1993).

15 Australian Fashion Council, *Fashion Evolution: From Farm to Industry Accelerating the Economic Impact of a Sector Powered by Women* (Ultimo, NSW: Australian Fashion Council, May 9, 2022), 15.

16 James Roberts, "Help the OR Foundation Stop Waste Colonialism," *FUTURE WORLD*, March 24, 2023.

17 Andrew Brooks et al., "Fashion, Sustainability, and the Anthropocene," *Utopian Studies* 28, no. 3 (2017): 493.

18 Otto von Busch, "'What Is to Be Sustained?': Perpetuating Systemic Injustices through Sustainable Fashion," *Sustainability: Science, Practice and Policy* 18, no. 1 (2022): 408.

19 Shannon Barbour, "Fashion Nova Answered Your Prayers and Is Selling a Meghan Markle Wedding Dress Replica for Dirt Cheap," *Cosmopolitan*, November 5, 2018. Available online.

20 Aja Barber, *Consumed: The Need for Collective Change: Colonialism, Climate Change & Consumerism* (New York: Hachette Book Group Inc., 2021), 61.

21 See Chioma Nadi, "Angelina Jolie Shakes Up Fashion with the Launch of Atelier Jolie," *Vogue*, September 27, 2023. Available online.

22 Sarah Manavis, "Preaching Sustainability While Hawking Fast Fashion—Meet the Greenwashing Influencers," *The Guardian*, December 11, 2023. Available online.

Chapter 2

1 Manzini and Jégou, *Sustainable Everyday*, 48.

2 John Thackara, *In the Bubble: Designing in a Complex World* (London and Cambridge, MA: The MIT Press, 2006), 29–30.

3 Thackara, *In the Bubble*, 188–9.

4 Parkins and Craig, *Slow Living,* 1.

5 Pauline Madge, "Design, Ecology, Technology: A Historiographical Review," *Journal of Design History* 6, no. 3 (1993): 150.

6 Tim O'Riordan, *Environmentalism (Research in Planning and Design)* (London: Pion, 1976).

7 Madge, "Design, Ecology, Technology," 149.

8 Ibid., 153.

9 Maurice Ash, *Green Politics: The New Paradigm* (London: The Green Alliance, 1980), mentioned in John Button (ed.) *A Dictionary of Green Ideas* (London and New York: Routledge, 1988), 193.

10 Nigel Whiteley, *Design for Society* (London: Reaktion Books Ltd, 1993), 53.

11 Whiteley, *Design for Society*, 91.

12 Madge, "Design, Ecology, Technology," 149.

13 Alice Payne, "Fashion Futuring in the Anthropocene: Sustainable Fashion as 'Taming' and 'Rewilding'," *Fashion Theory: The Journal of Dress, Body and Culture* 23, no. 1 (2019): 5–24.

14 Quoted in John Ehrenfeld and Andrew Hoffman, *Flourishing: A Frank Conversation about Sustainability* (Stanford, CA: Stanford University Press, 2015), 89.

15 Ehrenfeld and Hoffman, *Flourishing*, 128.

16 Victor Papanek, *The Green Imperative* (London: Thames & Hudson, 1995), 146.

17 Papanek, *The Green Imperative*, 17.

18 Alvin Toffler, *Future Shock* (New York and London: Bantam Books, 1970).

19 E. F. Schumacher, "Buddhist Economics," *Schumacher Center for a New Economics.* Available online.

20 Ehrenfeld in Kate Fletcher and Mathilda Tham (eds), *Routledge Handbook of Sustainable Fashion* (London: Routledge, 2015), 57.

21 McRobbie, "Second-Hand Dresses and the Role of the Ragmarket," in Angela McRobbie (ed.) *Zoot Suits and Second-Hand Dresses: An Anthology of Fashion and Music* (London: Macmillan, 1989), 48.

22 Deyan Sudjic, *Rei Kawakubo and Comme des Garçons* (New York: Rizzoli, 1990), 83.

23 Speaking in his biographical film of Yohji Yamamoto—*Notebook on Cities and Clothes*, directed by Wim Wenders, An Esicma Corporation, 1993, 1:21:00. VHS.

24 Dorinne Kondo, *About Face: Performing Race in Fashion and Theater* (New York and London: Routledge, 1997), 64.

25 Barbara Vinken, *Fashion Zeitgeist: Trends and Cycles in the Fashion System* (Oxford and New York: Berg, 2005), 143.

26 Chantal Fernandez, "Just Do It," *The Financial Times,* September 3, 2022, 25. Available online.

27 Richard Martin, "Exhibition Review: Yeohlee: Energetics: Clothes and Enclosures," *Fashion Theory: The Journal of Dress, Body & Culture* 2, no. 3 (1998): 293.

28 Vinken, *Fashion Zeitgeist*, 143.

29 Olivier Zahm, "Before and After Fashion," *Artforum* 33, no. 7 (1995): 74–7; Alison Gill, "Deconstruction Fashion: The Making of Unfinished, Decomposing and Re-Assembled Clothing," *Fashion Theory: The Journal of Dress, Body and Culture* 2, no. 1 (1998): 43.

30 Alison Gill, "Deconstruction Fashion: The Making of Unfinished, Decomposing and Re-Assembled Clothing," *Fashion Theory: The Journal of Dress, Body and Culture* 2, no. 1 (1998): 25–49, 35.

31 Amy M. Spindler, "Prince of Pieces," *The New York Times*, May 2, 1993.

32 Caroline Evans, "The Golden Dustman: A Critical Evaluation of the Work of Martin Margiela and a Review of Martin Margiela: Exhibition (9/4/1615)," *Fashion Theory: The Journal of Dress, Body and Culture* 2, no. 1 (1998): 81.

33 Vinken, *Fashion Zeitgeist*, 140.

34 Ibid., 150.

35 Kate Fletcher, "Slow Fashion: An Invitation for Systems Change," *Fashion Practice: The Journal of Design, Creative Process & The Fashion Industry* 2, no. 2 (2010): 259–65, 264.

36 Gill, "Deconstruction Fashion," 31.

37 Tom Pattinson, "The Wonders of Greta Thunberg: Read Our Interview with the Voice of a Generation," *Vogue Scandinavia*, August 8, 2021. Available online.

38 Emily Farra, "'Fashion Creates Culture and Culture Creates Action': Céline Semaan on the Industry's Role in Times of Crisis," *Vogue*, April 23, 2020. Available online.

39 Farra, *Vogue*, 11.

40 The Care Collective, *The Care Manifesto: The Politics of Interdependence* (London: Verso, 2020), 91.

41 Arturo Escobar, *Designs for the Pluriverse: Radical Interdependence, Autonomy, and the Making of Worlds* (Durham, NC: Duke University Press, 2018), 139.

42 Fiona Hackney et al., "Changing the World Not Just Our Wardrobes: A Sensibility for Sustainable Clothing, Care, and Quiet Activism," in Eugenia Paulicelli, Veronica Manlow, and Elizabeth Wissinger (eds) *The Routledge Companion to Fashion Studies* (Milton Park, UK: Taylor & Francis Group, 2021), 119.

43 Hackney et al., "Changing the World," 119.

Chapter 3

1 Manzini and Jégou, *Sustainable Everyday*, 16.

2 Caroline Evans, "End Times, Future Visions," in Kaat Debo, Alistair O'Neill, and Caroline Evans (eds) *Emotion: Fashion in Transition* (Tielt, Belgium: Lannoo Publishers, 2021), 131.

3 Elizabeth Wilson, *Adorned in Dreams, Fashion and Modernity* (London: Virago Press, 1985), 14.

4 John Thackara, "A Whole New Cloth: Politics and the Fashion System," in Kate Fletcher and Mathilda Tham (eds) *Routledge Handbook of Sustainable Fashion* (London and New York: Routledge, 2015), 43.

5 Kōhei Saitō, *Slow Down: The Degrowth Manifesto*, trans. Brian Bergstrom (New York: Astra House, 2024).

6 Timo Rissanen, "Possibility in Fashion Design Education—A Manifesto," *Utopian Studies* 28, no. 3 (2017): 537.

7 Philip B. Smith and Manfred Max-Neef, *Economics Unmasked: From Power and Greed to Compassion and the Common Good* (Totnes, UK: Green Books, 2011), 59.

8 Giles Lipovetsky, *The Empire of Fashion, Dressing Modern Democracy*, trans. Catherine Porter (Princeton, NJ: Princeton University Press, 1994), 5.

9 Kate Raworth, *Doughnut Economics, Seven Ways to Think Like a 21st Century Economist* (Vermont: Chelsea Green Publishing, 2017), 9.

10 The Care Collective, *The Care Manifesto: The Politics of Interdependence* (London: Verso, 2020), 73–4.

11 Ryann Devereaux, "Trayvon Martin's Parents Speak at New York March: 'Our Son Is Your Son'," *The Guardian*, March 22, 2012. Available online.

12 Marc Karimzadeh, "How Kerby Jean-Raymond is Helping COVID-19 Efforts," *CFDA*, March 19, 2020. Available online.

13 Miki Higasa, "1000 PPE Gown Production," *Fashion Girls for Humanity*, June 1, 2020. Available online.

14 Vogue, "Vogue Voices," *Vogue*, September 1, 2020, 157. Available online.

15 See Hazel Clark and Alla Eizenberg, "Yellow Socks," *Vestoj 11: On Everyday Life* (2023): 78–92.

16 Berg and Seeber, *The Slow Professor*, 71. Quoting Thomas Skovholt and Michelle Trotter-Mathison, *The Resilient Practitioner: Burnout Prevention and Self-Care Strategies for Counselors, Therapists, Teachers, and Health Professionals*, 2nd edn (London: Routledge/Taylor & Francis Group, 2011), 166.

17 Kipoz, *Slowness in Fashion*, 187.

18 In 2015, by fashion designer Alber Elbaz. Quoted in Agnès Rocamora, "Mediatization and Digital Media in the Field of Fashion," *Fashion Theory: The Journal of Dress, Body & Culture* 21, no. 5 (2017): 506.

19 Teresa Brennan, *The Transmission of Affect* (Ithaca, NY: Cornell University Press, 2004), 23. Quoted in Berg and Seeber, *The Slow Professor*, 38.

20 See Malcolm McCullough, *Abstracting Craft: The Practiced Digital Hand* (Cambridge, MA: MIT Press, 1996).

21 Heike Jenss, *Fashioning Memory: Vintage Style and Youth Culture* (London and New York: Bloomsbury, 2015).

22 Alex Esculapio, "Locating Emotionally Durable Fashion: A Practice-Based Approach" in Kipoz, *Slowness in Fashion*, 71.

23 Jonathan Chapman, "Prospect, Seed, and Activate: Advancing Design for Sustainability in Fashion," in Kate Fletcher and Mathilda Tham (eds) *Routledge Handbook of Sustainable Fashion* (London: Routledge, 2015), 79.

24 Anna Fitzpatrick and Kate Fletcher, *Research Project Note, Decentralizing Durability: Plural Ideas and Actions of Long Lasting Clothes* (London: Centre for Sustainable Fashion, University of the Arts, 2021), 14.

25 Fitzpatrick and Fletcher, *Research Project Note, Decentralizing Durability*, 25.

26 Anna König, "A Stitch in Time: Changing Cultural Constructions of Craft and Mending," *Culture Unbound: Journal of Current Cultural Research* 5, no. 4 (2013): 569–85.

27 Kate Sekules, *Mend!: A Refashioning Manual and Manifesto* (New York: Penguin Publishing Group, 2020) and IG @visiblemend.

28 The Collective, "Conversations of Decoloniality & Fashion," *Research Collective for Decoloniality & Fashion*; and Angela Jansen, "Fashion and the Phantasmogoria of Modernity: An Introduction to Decolonial Fashion Discourse," *Fashion Theory* 24, no. 6 (2020): 815–36.

29 A concept originating with the work of Stephen Greenblatt, *Renaissance Self-Fashioning: From Moore to Shakespeare* (Chicago, IL: University of Chicago Press, [1980] 2005).

30 Djurdja Bartlett, "The Politics of Transnational Fashion," *Fashion Theory: The Journal of Dress, Body and Culture* 26, no. 4 (2022): 459.

31 Descriptions are from the supporting catalog: Lidewij Edelkoort and Philip Fimmano, *Earth Matters June 10–November 26, 2017* (Netherlands: Textiel Museum, 2017).

32 Calvin Hui, "Dirty Fashion: Ma Ke's Fashion 'Useless,' Jia Zhangke's Documentary Useless and Cognitive Mapping," *Journal of Chinese Cinemas* 9, no. 3 (2015): 258.

33 Hui, "Dirty Fashion," 259.

34 Kate Fletcher, *Wild Dress: Clothing and the Natural World* (Axminster, UK: Uniformbooks, 2019).

35 Donna Haraway, *Staying with the Trouble: Making Kin in the Chthulucene* (Durham, NC: Duke University Press, 2016), 13.

36 Kate Fletcher and Mathilda Tham, *Earth Logic: Fashion Action Research Plan* (London: The JJ Charitable Trust, 2019), 27.

37 Amy Twigger Holroyd, Jennifer Farley Gordon, and Colleen Hill, *Historical Perspectives on Sustainable Fashion: Inspiration for Change* (London: Bloomsbury, 2023), 130.

38 Ma Ke, "Design with Conscience, Live with Simplicity" (unpublished lecture, Icograda World Design Congress, Beijing, October 28, 2009), 5. Available online.

39 Marco Pecorari, "The Fashion of the Manifesto," in Louise Wallenberg and Andrea Kollnitz (eds) *Fashion Aesthetics and Ethics: Past and Present* (London and New York: Bloomsbury Visual Arts, 2023), 91–108, 101.

40 Christopher Breward, "Foreword," in Heike Jenss (ed.) *Fashion Studies: Research Methods, Sites and Practices* (London and New York: Bloomsbury, 2016), xix–xx.

41 Timo Rissanen. “Possibility in Fashion Design Education—A Manifesto,” *Utopian Studies* 28, no. 3 (2017): 528–46, 530.

42 Rissanen, “A Manifesto,” 533.

43 Rissanen, “A Manifesto,” 537.

44 Sandra Niessen, “Defining Defashion: A Manifesto for Degrowth,” *International Journal of Fashion Studies* 9, no. 2 (2022), 439–44.

SELECTED FURTHER READING

Agins, Teri. *The End of Fashion: How Marketing Changed the Clothing Business Forever*, New York: William Morrow & Co, 1999.

Andrews, Cecile. *Slow Is Beautiful: New Visions of Community, Leisure and Joie de Vivre*, Canada: New Society Publishers, 2006.

Andrews, Geoff. *The Slow Food Story: Politics and Pleasure*, London: Pluto Press, 2008.

Barber, Aja. *Consumed: The Need for Collective Change: Colonialism, Climate Change & Consumerism*, New York: Hachette Book Group Inc., 2021.

Berg, Maggie and Barbara Seeber. *The Slow Professor: Challenging the Culture of Speed in the Academy*, Toronto; Buffalo; London: University of Toronto Press, 2016.

Brooks, Andrew. *Clothing Poverty: The Hidden World of Fast Fashion and Second-Hand Clothes*, London: Zed Books, 2019.

Buckley, Cheryl and Hazel Clark. *Fashion in Everyday Life: London and New York*, London and New York: Bloomsbury, 2017.

Button, John. *A Dictionary of Green Ideas: Vocabulary for a Sane and Sustainable Future*, London and New York: Routledge, [1988], 2019.

The Care Collective. *The Care Manifesto: The Politics of Interdependence*, London: Verso, 2020.

Carson, Rachel. *Silent Spring*, New York: First Mariner Books, [1962], 2002.

Clark, Hazel. "Slow + Fashion: An Oxymoron—or a Promise for the Future ...?" *Fashion Theory: The Journal of Dress, Body and Culture* 12, no. 4 (2008): 427–46.

Clark, Hazel. "Slow + Fashion—Women's Wisdom." *Fashion Practice: The Journal of Design, Creative Process and the Fashion Industry* 11, no. 3 (2019): 309–27.

Clark, Hazel and Alla Eizenberg. "Yellow Socks," *Vestoj 11: On Everyday Life* (2023): 78–92.

Cline, Elizabeth. *Overdressed: The Shockingly High Cost of Cheap Fashion*, New York: Portfolio/Penguin, 2012.

Cronberg, Anja Aronowsky. "Can Fashion Ever Be Democratic," *Vestoj*, January 13, 2010. Available online.

Debord, Guy. *The Society of the Spectacle*. Translated by Ken Knabb, Berkeley, CA: Bureau of Public Secrets, [1967], 2014.

de Certeau, Michel. "rf," in Gabrielle M. Spiegel (ed.) *Practicing History: New Directions in Historical Writing after the Linguistic Turn* (pp. 213–23), London and New York: Routledge, 2005.

Edelkoort, Lidewij. "Anti_Fashion: A Manifesto for the Next Decade," Paris: Trend Union, 2015.

Elkington, John. *The Green Consumer Guide: From Shampoo to Champagne: High-Street Shopping for a Better Environment*, London: Gollancz, 1989.

Escobar, Arturo. *Designs for the Pluriverse: Radical Interdependence, Autonomy, and the Making of Worlds*, Durham, NC: Duke University Press, 2018.

Evans, Caroline. "End Times, Future Visions," in Kaat Debo, Alistair O'Neill, and Caroline Evans (eds) *Emotion: Fashion in Transition* (pp. 130–55), Kasteelstraat, Belgium: Lannoo Publishers, 2021.

Evans, Caroline and Alessandra Vaccari, eds. *Time in Fashion: Industrial, Antilinear and Uchronic Temporalities*, London: Bloomsbury, 2020.

Fletcher, Kate. "Slow Fashion: An Invitation for Systems Change." *Fashion Practice: The Journal of Design, Creative Process & The Fashion Industry* 2, no. 2 (2010): 259–65.

Fletcher, Kate. "Slow Fashion," *The Ecologist*, 1 June 2007. Available online.

Fletcher, Kate. *Craft of Use: Post-Growth Fashion*, London and New York: Routledge, 2016.

Fletcher, Kate. *Wild Dress: Clothing and the Natural World*, Axminster, UK: Uniformbooks, 2019.

Fletcher, Kate and Mathilda Tham, eds. *Routledge Handbook of Sustainable Fashion*, London: Routledge, 2015.

Fletcher, Kate and Mathilda Tham. *Earth Logic: Fashion Action Research Plan*, London: The JJ Charitable Trust, 2019.

Fuad-Luke, Alastair. *Design Activism: Beautiful Strangeness for a Sustainable World*, London and New York: Earthscan, 2009.

Heti, Sheila, Heidi Julavitts, and Leanne Shapton. *Women in Clothes*, New York: Penguin Group, 2014.

Holroyd, Amy Twigger, Jennifer Farley Gordon, and Colleen Hill. *Historical Perspectives on Sustainable Fashion: Inspiration for Change*, London: Bloomsbury Publishing USA, 2023.

Honoré, Carl. *In Praise of Slowness: How a Worldwide Movement Is Challenging the Cult of Speed*. 1st edn, San Francisco, CA: Harper San Francisco, 2004.

Illich, Ivan. *Tools for Conviviality*, New York: Harper Collins, 1973.

Jansen, Angela. "Fashion and the Phantasmogoria of Modernity: An Introduction to Decolonial Fashion Discourse." *Fashion Theory: The Journal of Dress, Body & Culture* 24, no. 6 (2020): 815–36.

Jenss, Heike. *Fashioning Memory: Vintage Style and Youth Culture*, London and New York: Bloomsbury, 2015.

Kipoz, Şölen, ed. *Slowness in Fashion*, London: Dixi Books, 2020.

Kundera, Milan. *Slowness: A Novel* (translated by Linda Asher), New York: Perennial/Harper Collins, 1996.

Manzini, Ezio and François Jégou. *Sustainable Everyday: Scenarios of Urban Life*, Milan: Edizioni Ambiente, 2003.

Niessen, Sandra. "Defining Defashion: A Manifesto for Degrowth." *International Journal of Fashion Studies* 9, no. 2 (2022): 439–44.

Pais, Ana Paula and Carolyn F. Strauss, eds. *Slow Reader: A Resource for Design Thinking and Practice*, Amsterdam: Astrid Vorstermans, Valiz, 2016.

Palmer, Alexandra and Hazel Clark, eds. *Old Clothes New Looks Second Hand Fashion*, Oxford and New York: Berg, 2005.

Parkins, Wendy and Geoffrey Craig. *Slow Living*, Oxford and New York: Berg, 2006.

Petrini, Carlo. *Slow Food: The Case for Taste*. Translated by William McCraig, New York: Columbia University Press, 2001.

Raworth, Kate. *Doughnut Economics, Seven Ways to Think Like a 21st Century Economist*, Vermont: Chelsea Green Publishing, 2017.

Saitō, Kōhei (translated by Brian Bergstrom). *Slow Down: The Degrowth Manifesto*, New York: Astra House, 2024.

Schumacher, E. F. "Buddhist Economics." *Schumacher Center for a New Economics*, 1966. Available online.

Sekules, Kate. *Mend!: A Refashioning Manual and Manifesto*, New York: Penguin Publishing Group, 2020.

Toffler, Alvin. *Future Shock*, New York and London: Bantam Books, 1970.

Vinken, Barbara. *Fashion Zeitgeist: Trends and Cycles in the Fashion System*, Oxford and New York: Berg, 2005.

Von Busch, Otto. "'What Is to Be Sustained?': Perpetuating Systemic Injustices through Sustainable Fashion." *Sustainability: Science, Practice and Policy* 18, no. 1 (2022): 400–9.

Women's Earth Alliance. "What We Do." *WEA/Earth Island Institute*. Available online.

Woodward, Sophie. *Why Women Wear What They Wear*, Oxford and New York: Berg, 2007.

Žižek, Slavoj. *Living in the End Times*, London and New York: Verso, 2010.

INDEX